THE LITTLE

Heal Your Energy, Seek Enlightenment,

BOOK OF

and Deepen Your Understanding of

HERMETIC

Your Mind, Body, and Spirit

PRINCIPLES

AMBER D. BROWNE

Published by:
Ulysses Press
PO Box 3440
Berkeley, CA 94703
www.ulyssespress.com

ISBN: 978-1-64604-311-8
Library of Congress Control Number: 2021946539

Printed in the United States by Kingery Printing Company
10 9 8 7 6 5 4 3 2 1

Acquisitions editor: Claire Sielaff
Managing editor: Claire Chun
Project editor: Renee Rutledge
Editor: Kathy Kaiser
Front cover design: Chris Cote
Interior design: what!design @ whatweb.com
Production: Yesenia Garcia-Lopez
Artwork: © Science History Images/Alamy Stock Photo

This book is dedicated to my husband, Tristan,
for encouraging me to pursue my passion and purpose,
and to our awesome children, Mia and Dane,
for their constant acceptance and support.

CONTENTS

SECTION I

HERMES TRISMEGISTUS AND HERMETICISM.......................7

CHAPTER 1: INTRODUCTION 9

CHAPTER 2: WHO WAS HERMES TRISMEGISTUS? 11

CHAPTER 3: THE HISTORY OF HERMETICISM 15

CHAPTER 4: HERMES TRISMEGISTUS' WRITTEN WORKS............ 22

SECTION II

THE KYBALION—THE HERMETIC PRINCIPLES..................... 37

CHAPTER 5 *THE KYBALION* 39

CHAPTER 6 THE SEVEN HERMETIC PRINCIPLES 43

CHAPTER 7 PRINCIPLE 1: THE PRINCIPLE OF MENTALISM........... 46

CHAPTER 8 PRINCIPLE 2: THE PRINCIPLE OF CORRESPONDENCE... 69

CHAPTER 9 PRINCIPLE 3: THE PRINCIPLE OF VIBRATION 90

CHAPTER 10 PRINCIPLE 4: THE PRINCIPLE OF POLARITY 112

CHAPTER 11 PRINCIPLE 5: THE PRINCIPLE OF RHYTHM.............130

CHAPTER 12 PRINCIPLE 6: THE PRINCIPLE OF CAUSATION 151

CHAPTER 13 PRINCIPLE 7: THE PRINCIPLE OF GENDER 163

SECTION III

THE MYSTICAL TEACHINGS OF HERMES

TRISMEGISTUS...179

CHAPTER 14 ASTROLOGY... 181

CHAPTER 15 ALCHEMY...193

CHAPTER 16 MAGIC..204

CHAPTER 17 WE ARE ALL IN THIS TOGETHER............................ 211

BIBLIOGRAPHY..215

ACKNOWLEDGMENTS 220

ABOUT THE AUTHOR...224

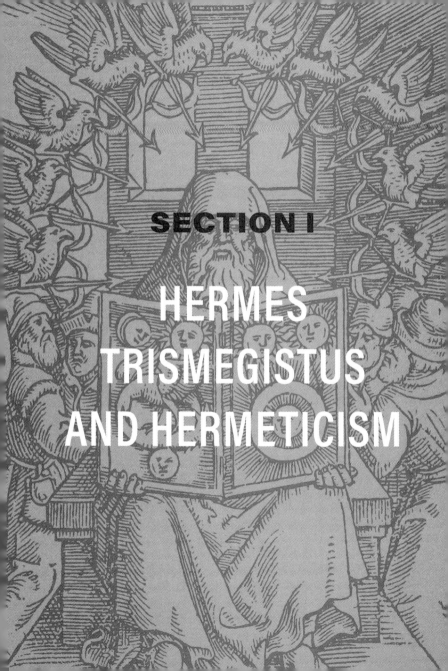

SECTION I

HERMES TRISMEGISTUS AND HERMETICISM

The allure of the unknown impels many to begin a journey toward mindfulness and enlightenment. Those who seek the meaning of life and their purpose in this world often grasp for knowledge through religion, the trial and error of life's events, meditation, or other means. *The Little Book of Hermetic Principles* delves into seven fundamental truths found throughout numerous cultures, religions, and belief systems across the globe and discusses how to incorporate these principles into your own life to discover your purpose and find fulfillment.

In this section, you will learn about the credited author of the Hermetic philosophy—Hermes Trismegistus, also known as the Thrice-Greatest—as well as the history and inner workings of Hermeticism, and a few of Trismegistus' written works. *The Kybalion,* published in 1908, breaks down Trismegistus' purported teachings into seven Hermetic principles, which are profound explanations of enlightenment and becoming one with God, or the One. *The Little Book of Hermetic Principles* outlines these principles and provides insight into incorporating this ancient knowledge into daily life. These principles guide a person toward enlightenment, or awareness—awareness between the self, others, and the natural world. Once you experience this awareness, you can then discover the true connectedness between everyone and everything on this planet and beyond.

Chapter 1

INTRODUCTION

This is a story about a man, a god, a priest, a sage—Hermes Trismegistus—and his purported writings and teachings. Hermeticism, attributed to Trismegistus, is an ancient body of knowledge that was passed down by word of mouth, from teacher to student, several millennia ago. The beliefs inherent to these teachings are included in a range of cultures and monotheistic religions across the globe. Many people believe in one true God, the Source, the Creator, or a higher power; many believe that everything happens for a reason and that there is no such thing as coincidence; and many believe that energy is an integral part of everything. *The Little Book of Hermetic Principles* delves into this ancient information and provides an easy-to-understand overview to the modern reader. It also explains how to come to a deeper understanding of the seven Hermetic principles, ultimately allowing yourself to heal your energy, seek enlightenment, and deepen your understanding of mind, body, and spirit.

In the beginning of the period that the Gregorian calendar calls the third millennium (the years 2001 to 3000), many have endured difficulty after difficulty. The COVID-19 pandemic and consequent worldwide turmoil have caused people to lose faith in humanity. Adults and children face challenges physically, mentally, and emotionally. Humanity must do better, and with this book, you can discover ancient information that might already hold a place in your belief system but might not be fully integrated into your psyche. *The Little Book of Hermetic Principles* will help you realize that although each person is an individual, everyone is in this life together, and all people are part of a greater plan—the bigger picture. This book shares the philosophical, religious, and scientific proof of these universal principles, all while helping you embark on a journey of self-discovery.

Chapter 2

WHO WAS HERMES TRISMEGISTUS?

Hermes Trismegistus, also known as the Thrice-Greatest, is credited with a number of ancient texts, which include philosophical, technical, and mystical teachings. Trismegistus is a mystery. Some believe he lived before the time of Moses. Others believe he was a succession of teachers or scribes who took the name to continue the philosophical work. Still others believe he never existed in human form on this earth. Most theorists have concluded, however, that Trismegistus lived in Egypt between 100 CE and 300 CE, but many of his philosophies were in practice for hundreds of years before his birth.

Hermetic philosophies are believed to have originated shortly after the age of Greek mythology. These philosophies first came to light in written word around 750 BCE, with accounts in Hesiod's poem *Theogony* and Homer's epics *The*

Iliad and *The Odyssey*. Trismegistus has been referred to as the Greek god Hermes, the god of communication, but also as the Egyptian god Thoth, god of knowledge and language, who was worshipped in Egyptian mythology several thousand years before Greek mythology was recognized.

How is it that one man is identified with two different deities? The Roman Empire conquered Egypt in 30 BCE, and the Romans allowed the existence and discussion of different religions of the time. Both the Greek god Hermes, later known in Roman mythology as Mercury, and the Egyptian god Thoth ruled over knowledge and communication, so these deities were associated with each other and with the author of the Hermetic writings. Trismegistus is ultimately known as a theologian and a philosopher. According to the preface written by translator John D. Chambers in *The Divine Pymander and Other Writings of Hermes Trismegistus*, Trismegistus "was considered to be the impersonation of the religion, art, learning, and sacerdotal discipline of the Egyptian priesthood."[1]

Texts accredited to Trismegistus were reportedly discovered sometime between 100 CE and 300 CE. They have been

1. Hermes Trismegistus, *The Divine Pymander and Other Writings of Hermes Trismegistus*, trans. John D. Chambers (Eastford, Connecticut: Martino Fine Books, 2018), vii.

translated numerous times over the past two thousand years. Manly P. Hall, Freemason and author of *The Secret Teachings of All Ages*, suggests Hermes Trismegistus was one of three things: a divinity accepted during the Greek period of Egyptian philosophy, a divinity represented by embodiments in priests, authors, and scribes of the time, or a ritualistic figure. Some early writers recognized Trismegistus as the deity of the universal mind. In a recorded lecture, Hall states that these writers "took the position that mind is the author of all works, therefore, that behind the human author of every product is the universal mind who might well therefore be regarded as the genuine compiler, writer, or editor of the work. Thus, a work could be dedicated to the universal mind as its true author."[2]

Although Trismegistus' written works do not refer to specific religions, they include the belief that everything is created by the Mind of God, and that within everything exists All-Father Mind, Life, and Light: "Whatever then doth live, oweth its immortality unto the Mind, and most of all doth

---

2. Manly P. Hall, 33rd degree Freemason, "The Hermetic Philosophy" (full lecture/clean audio), YouTube video, July 4, 2019, 7:04, MindPodNetwork, https://www.youtube.com/watch?v=P0LMh2bHNz0.

man, he who is both recipient of God, and co-essential with Him."[3]

Trismegistus' profound teachings were once secret, known only to those in power and to masters of Hermeticism. Today they are available to all who wish to learn. His writings on philosophy, science, the stars, and beyond are outlined in *The Little Book of Hermetic Principles*, giving you the opportunity to practice his teachings, whether he was a man or several men, an embodiment of a deity, or a deity or deities himself.

---

3. Hermes Trismegistus, *The Corpus Hermeticum: Initiation Into Hermetics, The Hermetica of Hermes Trismegistus,* trans. G. R. S. Mead (Pantianos Classics, 1906), 67.

Chapter 3

THE HISTORY OF HERMETICISM

Hermetic teachings enlighten those who are willing to learn about Trismegistus' philosophical principles, as well as about alchemy, astrology, and magic. The Thrice-Greatest is credited with recording ancient knowledge in texts such as *The Corpus Hermeticum* and *The Emerald Tablet of Hermes*, which have been translated throughout the centuries and are examined in this book.

The teachings of Trismegistus were once known only to those in power and to masters of Hermeticism. Trismegistus' written works were primarily translated from Greek during the medieval period, from the fifth century through the Renaissance (1400 CE to 1700 CE). Some of these earlier translations are stored in libraries worldwide, including in the Bodleian Library at the University of Oxford. In 1906,

Trismegistus' work *The Corpus Hermeticum*, translated by G. R. S. Mead, was published.

In 1908, *The Kybalion* was published. Written by an unknown author or authors with the pen name The Three Initiates, the work explores and explains the seven Hermetic principles, or the principles of mentalism, correspondence, vibration, polarity, rhythm, causation, and gender. (See Section II for a more detailed discussion of the seven Hermetic principles.) Some say the authors remained anonymous because the insight and information do not belong to them. *The Kybalion* became a modern explanation of Trismegistus' writings and influenced New Age ideas of mysticism and spirituality in the decades to come.

As humans continue to evolve, many people undergo life-altering transformations and shifts in beliefs in an effort to find meaning in this world. This was as true in ancient times as it is today. "When a nation conquered another nation, it conquered the gods along with mortals and brought its own religion, which superseded that of the people that had been conquered,"[4] states Hall in a recorded lecture. People worshipped based on the culture and the rulers of their time

---

4. Manly P. Hall, "The Hermetic Philosophy," 28:03.

and place. If rulers changed, then the faith changed to the new rulers' gods.

As the Roman Empire began conquering and ruling over many peoples, including those of Mediterranean and North African civilizations, Hall explains, religion was not imposed on those they had conquered. Instead, the Romans allowed them to keep their own beliefs; Egyptians, for example, maintained their belief system of gods and goddesses. According to Hall, this may have created an attitude shift, leading to sectarianism, or conflict often related to political or religious beliefs. As this attitude shift regarding ideologies and religious beliefs spread, people began to reject ideas they considered false or superstitious, which divided groups and caused many to question their own beliefs. Those living in or visiting areas conquered by the Roman Empire could educate themselves about various theologies and religions. Discussions and teachings led them to make their own philosophical and religious choices. The Romans, however, focused more on commerce and the economy. To the Romans, "religion was secondary to business."[5]

Individual intellectuality allowed Roman society to build philosophies and religions by taking beliefs from other cul-

5. Manly P. Hall, "The Hermetic Philosophy," 33:30.

Prior to 2500 BCE: Egyptian god Thoth is first recognized.	1400-1300 BCE: Moses is alive at some point during this period.		428/427-348/347 BCE: Plato lives during this period.	3rd century-1st century BCE: Greeks rule in Egypt.
	Prior to 1400 BCE: Some say Hermes Trismegistus lives during this period.	8th-7th century BCE: Ancient Greece reportedly sees the first written versions of Greek mythology, Hesiod's Theogony and Homer's *The Iliad and The Odyssey*.	384-322 BCE: Aristotle lives during this period.	

tures. This led to the rise of the work credited to Hermes Trismegistus, *The Corpus Hermeticum*. "It represents a natural instinct on the part of man, an instinct that we are feeling today, the instinct for the need for a substantial religious philosophy of life,"[6] Hall explains.

The rise of Christianity began in the first century CE and, according to Hall, the medieval church fathers recognized the truths of philosophers Trismegistus, Plato, and Aristotle. Instead of a polytheistic belief, which is the worship of many gods, the Hermetic philosophy is based on monotheism, the belief in one God. Some have described the Hermetic philosophy as pantheistic in the sense that one God, the Creator of all, lives within everything or that God is not an individual personality but is the universe. Similar beliefs in

---

6. Manly P. Hall, "The Hermetic Philosophy," 49:18.

1st century BCE: Romans conquer Egypt.	100–300 CE: Hermetic principles, initially passed down by word of mouth, are put into writing credited to Hermes Trismegistus.	1400–1700 CE: Renaissance; various translations of Hermes Trismegistus' writings appear.	1908 CE: *The Kybalion* is published.
1st century CE: Rise of Christianity.	**5th century–1400 CE:** Medieval era (Middle Ages); various translations of Hermes Trismegistus' writings appear.	**1687 ACE:** Sir Isaac Newton discovers/ identifies the law of universal gravitation and the laws of motion.	

religions and cultures across the globe point to one God, one Creator of all, as well as the power of the mind and the energy that exists within everything, which are outlined in the Hermetic principles. According to *The Kybalion*, the Hermetic teachings were primarily lost during the rule of Roman Emperor Constantine in the early fourth century with the rise of the Christian church. Trismegistus' writings would be kept alive by a few and translated throughout the medieval and renaissance periods. The Hermetic philosophy became increasingly popular in the early twentieth century with *The Kybalion*.

Although the Hermetic principles are not identified as such, many of these Hermetic beliefs, including the belief in a higher power, one true God, the Universe, the Source, and so on, who is responsible for all of creation, can be found in popular religions throughout history. According to *The Kybalion*, "The student of Comparative Religions will be able to perceive the influence of the Hermetic Teachings in every religion worthy of the name, now known to man, whether it be a dead religion or one in full vigor in our own times. There is always a certain correspondence in spite of the contradictory features, and the Hermetic Teachings act as the Great Reconciler."[7] In other words, basic truths such as the belief in one true Creator or living a pious life to become closer to this Creator exist in most religions across the globe. *The Kybalion* goes on to say, "The lifework of Hermes seems to have been in the direction of planting the great Seed-Truth which has grown and blossomed in so many strange forms, rather than establish a school of philosophy which would dominate the world's thought."[8] These truths included in Trismegistus' ancient teachings come, according to *The Kybalion*, "[w]hen the ears of the student are ready to hear."[9]

In ancient times of Greek and Roman civilizations, societies often flourished when inhabitants philosophized and spoke of ideas and beliefs. In current times, people might not

---

7. The Three Initiates, *The Kybalion: A Study of the Hermetic Philosophy of Ancient Egypt and Greece* (Chicago: The Yogi Publication Society, 1908), 9–10.

8. The Three Initiates, *The Kybalion*, 10.

9. The Three Initiates, *The Kybalion*, 12.

listen to all sides of the story, specifically when beliefs about religion, politics, and so on, are shared. If people in today's communities could return to having meaningful conversations and begin teaching and sharing information about the basic principles of life, then they could benefit from understanding the world and everyone in it.

Chapter 4

HERMES TRISMEGISTUS' WRITTEN WORKS

Trismegistus' written work is divided into two realms, the philosophical Hermetica which is considered more spiritual, and the technical Hermetica, which is considered more scientific and includes alchemy and astrology. Often, these realms coexist to lend a fuller understanding to the reader. *The Corpus Hermeticum* includes more of the philosophical side of the Thrice-Greatest's teachings, while *The Emerald Tablet of Hermes* and his written works about astrology, alchemy, and magic are known as his technical teachings.

The Kybalion teaches Trismegistus' work through seven Hermetic principles, which are apparent throughout the following reviewed books.

THE CORPUS HERMETICUM

The Corpus Hermeticum combines eighteen treatises, or short written works, credited to Hermes Trismegistus. *The Divine Pymander* is another translation of many of Hermes Trismegistus' written works included in *The Corpus Hermeticum*. *The Divine Pymander* includes translations of "Poemandres the Shepherd of Men" and thirteen other treatises credited to Trismegistus. The translations of these two books differ slightly, but the main ideas are similar.

The Corpus Hermeticum includes Trismegistus' philosophical Hermetica. Following are overviews of several sections included in *The Corpus Hermeticum*.

"POEMANDRES, THE SHEPHERD OF MEN"

The first section of *The Corpus Hermeticum*, "Poemandres, the Shepherd of Men," explains a mystical experience. Hermes Trismegistus receives a vision of Poemandres during meditation. Trismegistus questions who is calling out to him and receives the answer that He is the Man-Shepherd, or Poemandres, and is Mind. Trismegistus sees a vision that turns to light, which turns to darkness, which turns to nature, and then light again. "That Light," Poemandres states, "am I, thy God, Mind, prior to Moist Nature which appeared from Darkness; the Light-Word (Logos) [that appeared] from Mind is Son of God."[10] Poemandres continues, "So, understand the Light [He answered], and make friends with it."[11] No religious affiliation is mentioned in these writings by Trismegistus, but he states that God created All, that God is everything, and in everything is God.

Poemandres goes on to say, "Thou didst behold in Mind the Archetypal Form whose being is before beginning without end." In other words, God is the Creator of all, and is Mind, so from God's mind, all is created. He was in the universe before the beginning and created all, and all is within Him as He is within all. This refers to the Hermetic principle of mentalism, which will be discussed later in this book. "Poemandres, the Shepherd of Men" includes a discussion that through the will of God came the formation of the cosmos, the elements, nature, and fate. "From the downward elements Nature brought forth lives reason-less; for He did not extend the Reason (Logos) [to them]."[12] Poemandres explains

---

10. Trismegistus, *The Corpus Hermeticum*, 5.

11. Trismegistus, *The Corpus Hermeticum*, 5.

12. Trismegistus, *The Corpus Hermeticum*, 6.

that these "lives" without reason include things winged, things that swim, "four-footed things and reptiles, beasts wild and tame."[13]

During Poemandres' visit with Trismegistus, He asserts that "All-Father Mind, being Life and Light, did bring forth man co-equal to Himself, with whom He fell in love, as being His own child."[14] Poemandres says, "Nature thus brought forth frames to suit the form of man. And man from Light and Life changed into soul and mind—from Life to soul, from Light to Mind."[15] He states that man must live piously and be good, and those who gain gnosis, or spiritual understanding, will "be made one with God"[16] and be deathless. The spirit of a person is said to be living energy. A person should use this spiritual power for good, not evil, because those who are "impious" will never know God. Men have free will to choose good over evil, so those who choose to live a pious life will become one with God following physical death, when the body is surrendered and the energies ascend through various zones toward "the Father home."[17] In the translation titled *The Divine Pymander*, Poemander (called Poemandres

---

13. Trismegistus, *The Corpus Hermeticum*, 6.
14. Trismegistus, *The Corpus Hermeticum*, 6.
15. Trismegistus, *The Corpus Hermeticum*, 8.
16. Trismegistus, *The Corpus Hermeticum*, 11.
17. Trismegistus, *The Corpus Hermeticum*, 11.

in *The Corpus Hermeticum*), states, "This is the good ending of those attaining knowledge, to be made divine."[18] Following his vision of Poemandres, Trismegistus went on to spread his witnessed knowledge to others.

THE HERMETIC PRINCIPLES OF
THE CORPUS HERMETICUM

The remaining treatises of *The Corpus Hermeticum* include references to the Hermetic principles. The treatise "To Asclepius" includes a conversation between Hermes Trismegistus and Asclepius, who is believed to have been his student. Throughout the discussion, Trismegistus speaks of several principles, including vibration, to be discussed in Chapter 9, and causation, which will be addressed in Chapter 12. For example, Trismegistus asks if the mover has greater power than the moved. Asclepius affirms this notion. This refers to the Hermetic principle of causation outlined in *The Kybalion*, which states that every cause has an effect, and every effect has its cause. It is better to be the cause than the effect.

The Hermetic principle of vibration, which explains that everything, all matter, is in constant vibration because of

18. Trismegistus, *The Divine Pymander*, 14.

the atomic makeup of matter, is also mentioned. Asclepius questions Trismegistus' statement that nothing is void by pointing out such things as empty jars and cups. Trismegistus replies that air fills these empty receptacles, so they are not void. In other words, Trismegistus anticipates the discovery of atoms by saying that everything is something, even if that something cannot be seen with the naked eye. Vibration, or energy, is mentioned throughout *The Corpus Hermeticum*, including in a discussion between Trismegistus and Tat—thought to be either his son or his student—in "About the Common Mind." Trismegistus says that there is nothing in the universe that does not live. He continues, "For that the Father willed it should have Life as long as it should be."[19] Tat then questions the occurrence of death in all living things. Trismegistus replies, "They do not die, my son, but are dissolved as compound bodies. Now dissolution is not death, but dissolution of a compound; it is dissolved not so that it may be destroyed but that it may become renewed."[20] Energy is never created or destroyed. It simply changes form.

"Though Unmanifest God Is Most Manifest" in *The Corpus Hermeticum* has Trismegistus again speaking to Tat. Trismegistus refers to the Hermetic principle of mentalism, stating,

19. Trismegistus, *The Corpus Hermeticum*, 66.
20. Trismegistus, *The Corpus Hermeticum*, 66.

"Now 'thinking-manifest' deals with things made alone, for thinking-manifest is nothing else than making."[21] This principle states that creations in the physical plane come first from the mental plane and thoughts of the creator. Authors' thoughts become written words, painters' thoughts become art, chefs' thoughts become gourmet meals, and so on. The principle of mentalism is discussed later in this book.

"On Thought and Sense" in *The Corpus Hermeticum* discusses the physical and mental planes. "So sense and thought both flow together into man, as though they were entwined with one another. For neither without sensing can one think, nor without thinking sense."[22]

Throughout *The Corpus Hermeticum*, God, the Creator, is referred to as Good. Trismegistus writes that good thoughts are the seeds of God, and contradictory thoughts are "work of evil daimons."[23] Trismegistus states, "The greatest bad there is, is not to know God's Good"[24] and "The great ill of the soul is godlessness; then followeth fancy for all evil things and nothing good." [25] Trismegistus writes many times of free

---

21. Trismegistus, *The Corpus Hermeticum*, 27.

22. Trismegistus, *The Corpus Hermeticum*, 38.

23. Trismegistus, *The Corpus Hermeticum*, 38.

24. Trismegistus, *The Corpus Hermeticum*, 59.

25. Trismegistus, *The Corpus Hermeticum*, 61.

will. He states, "Mind, being Ruler of all things, and being Soul of God, can do whate'er it wills."[26]

Fate is also credited with man's undesirable choices. Trismegistus mentions the idea of karma in connection with fate. "It is fated, too, that he who doeth ill, shall suffer." [27] He goes on to say that those led by reason of the mind do not endure as much suffering as others. Trismegistus states that the gnosis, or understanding, of joy will force sorrow to flee, and often suggests singing praises and giving praise to God, the Good, the Father.

Trismegistus discusses the vastness of the cosmos and how nothing greater can exist. This is further examined in *The Kybalion*, which states that THE ALL created all and is in everything, and therefore nothing can exist outside THE ALL. *The Corpus Hermeticum* states, "He is the one of no body, the one of many bodies, nay, rather He of every body,"[28] referring to God. "The source and limit and the constitution of all things is God."[29]

---

26. Trismegistus, *The Corpus Hermeticum*, 63.

27. Trismegistus, *The Corpus Hermeticum*, 62.

28. Trismegistus, *The Corpus Hermeticum*, 30.

29. Trismegistus, *The Corpus Hermeticum*, 37.

THE EMERALD TABLET OF HERMES

Most scholars know *The Emerald Tablet of Hermes*, or the technical Hermetica, includes mostly technical writings credited to Hermes Trismegistus, but this work also includes some of the philosophical principles discussed later in this book. *The Emerald Tablet of Hermes*, basically a list of numbered statements about one page in length, is said to be a blueprint for the study of alchemy and the creation of the philosopher's stone. Alchemy is a predecessor to chemistry. Some of the practices, techniques, and tools used in alchemy in ancient times are still used today. Those who initially practiced alchemy did so in secret, sharing formulas via symbols that only other alchemists could understand. The alchemists' main goals were to change metal into gold by way of "magic," or transmutation of matter, and to create the philosopher's stone, which was thought to give eternal life.

The secrets within *The Emerald Tablet of Hermes* were translated over the centuries. Most of the translations are similar, categorizing the writings into as many as fourteen distinct statements, with minor differences among the translations due to the evolution of languages spoken at the time of translation. One translator, Helena Blavatsky, also known as Madame Blavatsky, states in general commentary regarding

The Emerald Tablet of Hermes that "the universal, magical agent, the astral light, which in the correlations of its forces, furnishes the alkahest, the philosopher's stone, the elixir of life."[30] Blavatsky goes on to say that Hermetic philosophy identifies this "universal, magical agent" as "the soul of the world." Finding the philosopher's stone to bring eternal life and cure ailments was a goal of early alchemists. So it could be concluded that if alchemists could gain control of this "astral light," they would be able to create the philosopher's stone. Following are translated examples of and additional commentary regarding the statements of Hermes Trismegistus included in *The Emerald Tablet of Hermes*.

From Fulcanelli, translated from French, "1) This is the truth, the whole truth and nothing but the truth."[31] This phrase is often used in courtrooms by those about to testify on the stand and, according to Trismegistus, the statement references that the remainder of the text should be taken as truth. "2) That which is above is from that which is below, and that which is below is from that which is above, working the miracles of one,"[32] is the translation by Jabir ibn Hayyan. In commentary regarding this truth of *The Emerald*

30. Hermes Trismegistus, *The Emerald Tablet of Hermes,* trans. by multiple translators (Los Angeles: Merchant Books, 2013), 35.

31. Trismegistus, *Emerald Tablet,* 20.

32. Trismegistus, *Emerald Tablet,* 7.

Tablet of Hermes, the philosopher known as Hortulanus states that the philosopher's stone is divided into two parts: "[T]he inferior part is earth which is called nurse and ferment, and the superior part is the spirit which quickens the whole stone and raises it up. Wherefore separation made, and conjunction celebrated, many miracles are affected."[33] As above, so below, and vice versa is discussed in *The Kybalion* as the principle of correspondence, meaning the same truths exist on all planes—physical, mental, and spiritual.

From the alleged Phoenician translation of Kriegsmann, "3) And as the whole universe was brought forth from one by the word of one God, so also all things are regenerated perpetually from this one according to the disposition of Nature."[34] It can thus be concluded that all things come from the Creator, and all things will always come from this one Creator.

The fourth statement of the text states that the father is the sun and the mother the moon. According to commentary by Titus Burckhardt, the sun "is the spirit (nous), while the moon is the soul (psyche)."[35] Regarding this notion, the moon is associated with water and the sun with fire, so according to commentary by a person referred to only as Schumaker in

33. Trismegistus, *Emerald Tablet*, 25.
34. Trismegistus, *Emerald Tablet*, 15.
35. Trismegistus, *Emerald Tablet*, 27.

the text, "the *prima materia* is understood to have been generated by fire, born of water, brought down from the sky by wind, and nourished by the earth."[36] One belief held by early alchemists was that matter is made of four elements—earth, water, air, and fire. This is no longer accepted as truth. Today, chemists have discovered more than one hundred elements, which form different states of matter. The common states of matter—solid, liquid, gas, and plasma—could be considered closely related to alchemists' theories.

Several translations of the fifth statement reference that the wind bore the secret to it, possibly referring to the philosopher's stone, in its belly, while the earth nursed it. The sixth statement says everything on this earth comes from it, and it's power is perfect.

It appears that the seventh statement in translations refers to the process of alchemy. Trismegistus' statement discusses separating earth from fire, "the subtle and thin from the crude and course,"[37] according to the translation from Georgio Beato, the *Aurelium Occultae Philosophorum*. Commentary from Sigismund Bacstrom refers to this process as

---

36. Trismegistus, *Emerald Tablet*, 27.
37. Trismegistus, *Emerald Tablet*, 12.

distillation, while Schumaker states that the prime matter must be fixed into a substance so that it may be handled.

From Madame Blavatsky's translation comes this statement: "8) Ascend with the greatest sagacity from earth to heaven, and unite together the power of things inferior and superior."[38] Commentary describes this technical truth of Trismegistus as a distillation process, possibly relating to alchemy. The remaining technical statements in *The Emerald Tablet of Hermes* include Idres Shah's translation, "9) Thus you will have the illumination of all the world, and darkness will disappear."[39] Translation commentary concludes that this means the stone can provide insight, and according to Burckhardt, "The light of the Spirit becomes constant [and] ignorance, deception, uncertainty, doubt, and foolishness will be removed from consciousness,"[40] with the person following these precepts thus becoming closer to or one with God. The tenth statement of *The Emerald Tablet* translations refer to it, possibly the philosopher's stone, as all-powerful and able to overcome the subtle and penetrate the solid. The eleventh goes on to say that this is how the world was created. As for the twelfth technical statement, "from this are

---

38. Trismegistus, *Emerald Tablet,* 19.

39. Trismegistus, *Emerald Tablet,* 22.

40. Trismegistus, *Emerald Tablet, 33.*

born marvelous adaptations," the means to achieve it are mentioned in the text.

In the recognized thirteenth statement, Trismegistus refers to himself as having three parts of this philosophical knowledge. Burckhardt comments that these three parts are basically the physical, mental, and spiritual realms, while Schumaker proclaims Trismegistus to be the "greatest philosopher, the greatest priest, and the greatest king,"[41] thus the Thrice-Greatest. Most translations conclude with a fourteenth statement which basically refers to the previous statements as the completed work of the sun.

The Emerald Tablet of Hermes is said to include the wisdom of the entire universe. Although the philosopher's stone never materialized for these ancient alchemists, they discovered practices, tools, and techniques during their studies that are still used today. These alchemists are often credited with paving the way for modern-day chemists.

---

41. Trismegistus, *Emerald Tablet*, 35.

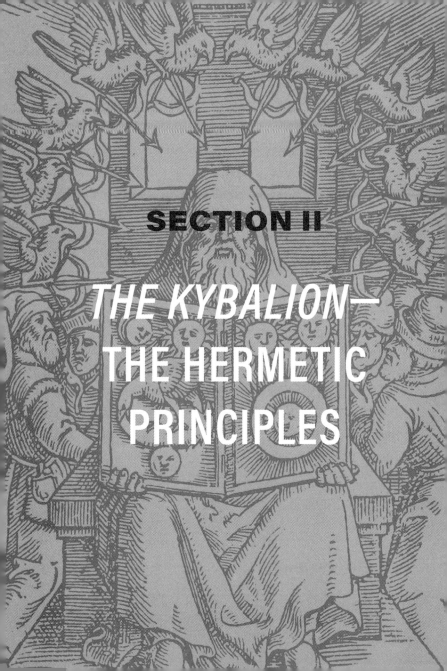

SECTION II

THE KYBALION—
THE HERMETIC PRINCIPLES

The Kybalion categorizes the seven Hermetic principles purportedly written by Hermes Trismegistus. Published by the Yogi Publication Society in 1908, *The Kybalion* is a philosophical look at these basic principles, or laws, evident in global religions and belief systems. No one has been able to confirm the identities of those who actually wrote *The Kybalion* because the authors refer to themselves only as "The Three Initiates." They explain each of the seven Hermetic principles and how they manifest in daily life. These principles are interconnected, and those willing to educate themselves can use these "laws" to become more enlightened and aware of themselves and the world around them.

In this section, an overview of *The Kybalion* is provided and the Hermetic principles explained. Experts, ranging from therapists and professors to scientists and yogis, share how they see and interact with these principles each day and how readers can incorporate these ancient truths into their lives.

Chapter 5

THE KYBALION

The Kybalion explains Trismegistus' philosophies and how wisdom is received only "[w]hen the ears of the student are ready to hear."[42] Although many of the Hermetic teachings were intended only for groups studying Hermeticism and for the illumed, or the enlightened, *The Kybalion* states, "The possession of Knowledge, unless accompanied by a manifestation and expression in Action, is like the hoarding of precious metals—a vain and foolish thing. Knowledge, like Wealth, is intended for Use."[43] The Hermetic philosophy includes teachings such as, all things exist because the One created all; in everything, the Creator exists; and nothing is ever at rest but instead is in constant vibration.

Gaining popularity throughout the 1900s and early 2000s, *The Kybalion* has been discussed and reviewed by many scholars and laypeople alike, all wanting to learn more about

---

42. The Three Initiates, *The Kybalion*, 12.
43. The Three Initiates, *The Kybalion*, 213.

the ancient Egyptian and Greek knowledge and how it can be incorporated into daily life to bring a greater self-awareness and understanding of reality.

The Kybalion states that someone who studies Hermeticism should continue to study the scientific views of the universe, as well as understand the principle of mentalism, which states, "THE ALL is Mind; the Universe is Mental—held in the Mind of THE ALL."[44] The principle of mentalism, in relation to the principle of correspondence ("As above, so below; as below, so above")[45] can be difficult to understand. However, one must come to understand that art, structures, clothing, and so on, come first from the mind of the human creator and ultimately from the mind of THE ALL. All things created in nature exist because of THE ALL. Everything first existed in the mind of THE ALL and then became reality, just as a screenwriter first creates a mental understanding of a fictional character, and then this character "comes to life" on-screen. The character exhibits traits specific to that personality, but part of the creator still exists within the character. Will the character ever become the creator? No,

---

44. The Three Initiates, *The Kybalion*, 90.
45. The Three Initiates, *The Kybalion, 28.*

but the creator will always be part of the character because that character was "born" in the mind of the creator.

The Kybalion states, "While All is in THE ALL, it is equally true that THE ALL is in All. To him who truly understands this truth hath come great knowledge."[46] *The Kybalion* offers this example: "THE ALL is in the earth-worm, and yet the earth-worm is far from being THE ALL."[47] Although THE ALL is part of the earthworm, the earthworm will never be THE ALL, for THE ALL is unknowable and infinite. But THE ALL—the Source, the Creator, God, and so on—is part of each person and everything in the universe and in fact is the Universe.

The authors of *The Kybalion* say Hermetic thought influenced the early philosophers of Greece, who were responsible for the foundation of modern scientific theory. Although the principle of mentalism states that everything in the universe is "mental," *The Kybalion* says that "the Universe and its laws, and its phenomena, are just as REAL, so far as Man is concerned."[48] It goes on to state that because the universe is in a constant state of change, it is devoid of reality. But humans

---

46. The Three Initiates, *The Kybalion*, 95.

47. The Three Initiates, *The Kybalion*, 99.

48. The Three Initiates, *The Kybalion*, 90.

"are compelled to ACT AND LIVE as if the fleeting things were real and substantial."[49] So although everything and everyone is said to have been created in the mind of THE ALL, humans exist in this reality and must continue to learn and grow to ultimately reach a higher level of understanding and consciousness.

---

49. The Three Initiates, *The Kybalion*, 91.

Chapter 6

THE SEVEN HERMETIC PRINCIPLES

Although separate, the seven Hermetic principles outlined in *The Kybalion* work together to foster a better understanding of reality, how the universe works, and the interconnectedness of everything. These seven principles can be found in various religions and belief systems across the globe, and they are similar to a number of universal laws, which are generally accepted as truth. The Hermetic principles of correspondence, vibration, and causation are considered universal laws, as is the law of compensation, which is mentioned in *The Kybalion* but not identified as one of the seven Hermetic principles.

1. The principle of mentalism: All is mind.

2. The principle of correspondence: Planes exist—body, mind, and spirit.

3. The principle of vibration: Everything is energy.

4. The principle of polarity: Everything is a degree of its opposite.

5. The principle of rhythm: The pendulum of life swings.

6. The principle of causation: Everything is either a cause or an effect.

7. The principle of gender: Masculine and feminine energies exist in all.

These Hermetic principles work together in every aspect of life. One law that has gained more acknowledgment in recent years—due to the popularity of the book and documentary *The Secret*—is the law of attraction. It appears that many of the Hermetic principles are at work in the law of attraction, which states that thoughts can be manifested into reality. The principle of mentalism is incorporated in the law of attraction, in that all creation comes from the mind, specifically, the mind of THE ALL. The principle of vibration, which states that everything and everyone is vibration, or energy, is incorporated in the law of attraction: energy attracts energy. The principle of causation, which states that everything is a cause or an effect, reflects the law of attraction. For example, if someone takes action on a thought, that action leads to a result, and so on.

The following chapters review Trismegistus' Hermetic teachings as explained in *The Kybalion* and describe how these truths can be discovered in daily life and beyond.

Chapter 7

PRINCIPLE 1: THE PRINCIPLE OF MENTALISM

Whether you think you can, or you think you can't—you're right.
—Henry Ford, founder of Ford Motor Company

"It's all in your head." Sometimes this phrase can lend courage to someone who isn't sure whether to take a risk, such as jumping off the high dive at the local pool. In a different situation, these words might help a dreamer understand that the shadow in the corner seen upon waking from a nightmare is imaginary, an illusion created by the mind. But for the diver feeling the fear of smacking the water below or the dreamer waking in a panic, these "all in your head" bits of reality evoke real feelings and emotions. The principle of mentalism explains that events, feelings, and so on, may come true for people based on their perceptions of reality, their thoughts. *The Kybalion* states that everything created in the mind of THE ALL, from the sand on the beach to the stars above and beyond, is real because the finite mind of the person believes it is real. Reality is based on perception. Does this mean that if you believe you can fly and jump off a roof, you will go soaring into the night sky? No. Other laws come into play, such as the law of gravity. Does this mean if you believe a mouse is a house, the mouse becomes a house because of your perception? No. Other principles are at work. "We do not live in a world of dreams, but in a Universe which, while relative, is real so far as our lives and actions are concerned. Our business in the Universe is not to deny its existence, but to LIVE, using the Laws to rise from lower to higher—living on, doing the best that we can under the circumstances arising each day, and living, so far as is possible, to our highest ideas and ideals."[50]

The principle of mentalism focuses on perception: everything is possible if a person believes it is possible. Although Hermeticism is not a specific religion, the teachings of the Hermetic philosophy are seen in multiple belief systems and religions around the world. In the New Testament, Mark 11:24 alludes to the principle of mentalism: "Therefore I say

---

50. The Three Initiates, *The Kybalion*, 92–93.

unto you, What things soever ye desire, when ye pray, believe that ye receive them, and ye shall have them."[51]

Does this mean that if a person really believes they will land a date with a certain celebrity this weekend that it will happen? Not necessarily. Events happen according to law. What a person believes and works toward might not happen at that precise moment or at any time in the future, but it might. And if not, then it was not meant to be at that time in a person's life, which could refer to the principle of causation, which states that everything happens as stated by law and that nothing happens by chance. But if a person does not receive what is desired, something better is on its way and will make itself known at the moment that it is meant to happen.

THE ALL is MIND; The Universe is Mental.
—The Kybalion

The Kybalion states that the Hermetic principle of mentalism "explains the true nature of 'Energy,' 'Power,' and 'Matter,' and why and how all these are subordinate to the Mastery of the Mind."[52] It points out that an old Hermetic master

---

51. *The Holy Bible, King James Version* (Nashville, Tennessee: Thomas Nelson Publishers, 1989), 837.
52. The Three Initiates, *The Kybalion*, 28.

wrote, "He who grasps the truth of the Mental Nature of the Universe is well advanced on The Path to Mastery."[53] If you understand the Hermetic teachings of "mental transmutation," or changing and transforming thoughts into other forms, then you can create reality. *The Kybalion* states that when a person focuses on the unreality of things, they ignore the practical work. Instead, a person should "use Law against Laws; the higher against the lower; and by the Art of Alchemy transmute that which is undesirable into that which is worthy, and thus triumph."[54] What does this statement mean? Learn to vibrate at a higher frequency—that is, escape pain by rising to a higher awareness—and remember that "transmutation, not presumptuous denial, is the weapon of the Master."[55] Transmutation, or change, is inevitable, so one should work with this fact instead of against it.

Those who seek knowledge, listen to intuition, and practice finding their higher selves are on a path to their greatest good, "and the road leads upward ever."[56]

---

53. The Three Initiates, *The Kybalion*, 28.

54. The Three Initiates, *The Kybalion*, 92.

55. The Three Initiates, *The Kybalion*, 92.

56. The Three Initiates, *The Kybalion*, 93.

THE POWER OF THE MIND

The mind is a very complex creation. If a person's thoughts are inspirational and positive, then that person's emotions and physical actions and reactions will follow suit. Instead of focusing on worry, doubt, or fear, a person should learn to appreciate each moment of life, even if at first a particular moment causes a negative or unbeneficial physical, mental, emotional, or spiritual response. Mentalism is a key component of a positive mindset and change of attitude. If someone has a desire to reach a goal, that person is motivated to work and improve to ultimately reach that goal. Anything is possible!

Every person on this planet has thoughts moving through the mind all day and all night. The mind never stops working. It is a powerful machine that can be used as a benefit or a hindrance, depending on a person's frame of mind and level of physical, emotional, and spiritual well-being. Changing the mind is not an easy process. For some, it could seem impossible because they think they cannot change negative habits, they do not know how to change, they fear what comes after achieving a goal, or they simply do not want to make the effort to increase awareness about the possibilities of this life.

With the amount of motivational, inspirational, and therapeutic videos, memes, articles, books, classes, sessions, and so on, available, anyone can learn and strive to be a better person if one chooses to do so. Everyone faces hardships. It is the power of the mind and the ability to control thoughts and emotions that allow a person to overcome challenges, continue growth, and move forward in life. Help is available. But you must make a conscious effort to use these tools and techniques, continuing to develop habits that will lead to better outcomes.

If the mind believes something is achievable, the possibilities are endless. Renowned physicist Albert Einstein said, "Imagination is everything. It is the preview of life's coming attractions." The imagination can lead to the creation of a tangible form of the imagined. Thoughts lead to manifestation. However, thoughts of worry, anxiety, sadness, ungratefulness, and so on, do not *have* to lead to manifestation. A person who has trained the mind to acknowledge these thoughts—which can lead to negative emotional and physical reactions—and then release them, thus moving on to a more positive and thankful mindset, can manifest more positive and beneficial aspects of life. Despite hardship, many in today's world have overcome setbacks and created better lives for themselves. It is possible, but it takes work, support, and determination. Do not give up. Instead, put in the work and make the changes necessary to create a better reality.

MOTIVATIONAL AND INSPIRATIONAL QUOTES

✳ "You have something special. You have greatness in you. You have the ability to create wealth. You have the ability to make an impact. You have the ability to make a difference."[57]—Les Brown, motivational speaker

✳ "God didn't put it in their imagination. He put it in yours. It was your evidence of things not seen. See, all this stuff you've been imagining, you ought to start working on it 'cause that's what God really got for you. Your real life is in your imagination."[58]—Steve Harvey, entertainer, motivational speaker

✳ "Wherever focus goes, energy flows....You may have dreamed about it, thought about it, talked about it, but when you focus on something continuously, something

57. Les Brown, *Success* magazine, "The Story You Believe About Yourself Determines Your Success," YouTube video, October 8, 2017, 22:38, https://www.youtube.com/watch?v=68Wz25NMX2k.

58. Steve Harvey, The Official Steve Harvey, "Imagination Is Everything,"YouTube video, June 10, 2019, 3:12, https://www.youtube.com/watch?v=TbEMIw3ecGI.

magical happens. You get insights."[59]—Tony Robbins, motivational speaker

WAYS TO GROW AND UNDERSTAND THE MIND

In today's world, a plethora of information to aid mental growth is available at the click of a button. Whether it is an inspirational YouTube video, an uplifting meme on social media, or an article about how to have a more positive mindset, the information is out there for all to use.

With so much information available, where can you begin the journey to awareness, education, and enlightenment? Start by discovering a goal. The goal could be to have a more positive outlook on life. It could be to learn a new skill. Or the goal could be building more meaningful relationships. Whatever the goal, it is possible to attain it if you believe it is possible and put in the work to achieve it. It takes time but anything can happen.

---

59. Tony Robbins, "Where Focus Goes, Energy Flows," YouTube video, January 17, 2017, 1:26, https://www.youtube.com/watch?v=Z6nv26BTzKA.

There is the unconfirmed notion that when the universe puts a thought out into the world, someone is going to think this thought and do what it takes to make it a reality. So if motivation strikes a person, then that person should grab it and go with it. If someone believes it is possible, then it is possible.

Perception is a huge part of the mind. When someone thinks a certain way or is instilled with a specific ideal, that person might not be open to changing this perception. Different people might have a different view of a specific person or event based on perception. Whether it is the details of an accident that they witnessed, the takeaway theme of a book or movie, or the motives of another person, these beliefs and thoughts are based on personal experience, preconceived ideas, prejudices, and so on. An open mind allows a person to view all the facts of a situation objectively, and it allows that person to make unbiased and unprejudiced decisions in all aspects of life.

CHANGING A MINDSET

Growth mindset vs. fixed mindset is a concept that has been embraced by the corporate world and educational institutions in recent years. Carol Dweck, PhD, psychologist at

Stanford University, first used these two terms in her book *Mindset: The New Psychology of Success*. Many business leaders and teachers have implemented these strategies in training employees or teaching students, educating them on how to change their way of thinking so that it is more productive.

The person with a growth mindset thinks success is possible with education and effort. Most athletes have a growth mindset when it comes to their sport. They practice for hours each day, refuse to give up on their dreams, and continue to improve physically and mentally to reach their goals. Some people have a growth mindset regarding certain skills but have a fixed mindset regarding other skills. For example, a writer might believe that education and experience will improve their writing—but believe that because they haven't managed to lose weight so far, they never will take off and keep off extra pounds. The person with a fixed mindset believes that regardless of how much they try, they will never succeed. They think their current reality will never change because that is how it has always been.

To change your way of thinking, you can become more aware of your personal and professional goals and what it might take to reach these goals. According to the Hermetic principle of mentalism, if a person truly believes it is possible, then a goal could become a reality. It may take years to develop a certain skill and years more to hone that skill to succeed at a goal. The goal, however, might never be accomplished. If this happens, the person with a growth mindset might change course and develop a new goal, ultimately keeping the determination and the faith that they are or will be successful.

Is changing a mindset easy? It depends. If a person already has a growth mindset in one area of life, then it may be a little easier for that person to develop this mindset in other areas. If a person has always felt stuck in situations with no way out, it will take time to develop a different outlook. Listening to inspirational speeches, keeping a positive outlook, raising self-awareness, reaching out for support, and so on, can help a person gain guidance about what they want to accomplish in this life—and the confidence that they can.

EXERCISE BENEFITS MORE THAN JUST PHYSICAL PERFORMANCE

Exercising the body can lead to a lean and muscular physique, but the act of moving the body to increase heart rate and strength yields more benefits than just physical improvements. Mendy Samman, master black belt in American karate and master personal trainer, believes exercise is even more important for a person's mental health and brain health than their physical health. "Exercise provides more blood to your brain. It releases more feel-good hormones, helps you to relax throughout your day, and deal with everyday stress."

The power of the mind plays an important role in exercise. Many people hesitate to start their journey to physical fitness because they fear the unknown, have possible physical constraints, or just "don't have the time." Taking small steps toward a healthier lifestyle can help alleviate the self-doubt and self-sabotage. "We put limitations on ourselves that really don't exist because we don't want to fail or because somebody else said we were already a failure," Samman states. She suggests people find an exercise that makes them feel excited and fits their personality. "If you were a dancer as a child, you may feel connected to that particular type of exercise," Samman suggests, referencing barre classes, which implement ballet. "If you like fighting and you watch fighting on TV," she shares, "then boxing or kickboxing may be an exercise that makes you feel empowered."

For Samman, who suffered a brain injury as a child due to a dirt bike accident, brain health has been a huge benefit of exercise. "I've seen significant improvement in my ability to concentrate, think clearly, and retain information when I exercise versus when I have to sit all the time," she explains.

Exercise helped increase Samman's reaction times when she competed in professional, full-contact kickboxing. "It was extremely challenging to my body....Weight lifting, exercise, and cardio definitely helped me to perform at a higher level, to think faster, to move my body faster, to avoid getting hit." She also competed in American karate. "That's fun too. It helps your brain to click faster, to make the connections faster into your body, so you respond better. You have a better reaction time, so that even reflects into your driving and everyday activities."

Of course, exercise helps a person be more physically fit, which can improve balance and keep them from getting tired doing everyday activities. It also helps eliminate pain, such as hip, back, neck, or shoulder pain, which can be caused by sitting most of the day at work or home. Exercise improves heart health, lowers the percentage of body fat, reduces cholesterol, and helps ward off diabetes and kidney failure. "It's all linked," Samman says. "To me, weight lifting is the most beneficial because you can get bone health, heart health, strength, [and] lose weight."

A favorite cardio workout for Samman is boxing, which makes running and lifting weights easier. "If you are a sprinter, your heart works one way. If you are a long-distance runner, your heart works another way. So with boxing, you can kind of hit both ways your heart works, so you get both benefits—endurance and explosion work."

The type of exercise you choose—whether yoga, kickboxing, weight lifting, running, or playing in a softball or volleyball league—depends on your physical capabilities. Finding a partner, class, or trainer to uphold accountability will not only increase the desire to get out there and exercise, but also help build a connection with another person. Before you join a class or hire a personal trainer, do your research to make sure the teacher or trainer has the necessary qualifications and experience. Samman suggests that, regardless of workout experience, you continue to increase your own knowledge about anatomy and how muscles and joints work. "This helps you feel more knowledgeable when you do go to a trainer or start a new class. You know how your body is moving." If you understand your body, you will be able to identify whether you feel discomfort because you are sore from working new muscles or if you have suffered an injury.

When it comes to exercise, anything is better than nothing. "I think everybody needs to be active for at least 30 minutes every day. Ideally, I think you need to be out moving around for at least an hour every day." She suggests splitting the workout time. For example, a person can walk 15 to 30 minutes at lunch and add 30 minutes of walking in the morning or evening. Exercising earlier in the day is an added benefit because it boosts metabolism throughout the day.

For those new to working out, Samman suggests beginning with a simple exercise. "It's a 1-minute goal. That's all you have to do." Marching or getting up and sitting back down while watching television can be a first step. Doing squats in the kitchen while waiting for your tea to brew can also be a start to incorporating exercise into your daily routine. "Pretty soon you're outside walking," Samman says. A short exercise time allows you to become more comfortable over time, adding more exercise for longer periods as you progress. "I think the biggest thing that people don't like is feeling out of breath. It's uncomfortable when you feel like you can't breathe. So once someone is sweating, or they're huffing, it becomes almost a panic, so they don't want to do it anymore." If a person starts with a simple exercise routine and continues to add more over time, healthier results begin to happen, boosting physical, mental, and emotional effects. "It's all connected."

TAKEAWAYS

1. Find an exercise or workout program that instills excitement.

2. Find a partner, trainer, team, or class to uphold accountability.

3. Start small but keep moving and increasing exercise in small increments.

4. Exercise at least 30 minutes each day.

5. Do not give up; it gets easier as you build endurance and habit.

POWER OF THE MIND: VISION BOARDS

A vision board gives the person envisioning the desired future a visual reminder of their dreams and goals. These visual representations of your dreams and goals can motivate and inspire you to do what it takes to fulfill them. Seeing these visual representations daily can help you manifest them into reality. A vision board can include pictures, quotes, reminders, and so on, regarding relationships, mental and emotional growth, physical wellness, possessions, and so on.

HOW TO CREATE A VISION BOARD

1. Identify and create a list of dreams and goals to include on the vision board.

2. Purchase a poster, cork board, or other display to attach visual reminders.

3. Cut out photos from magazines that allude to the dreams and goals.

4. Write out or print affirmations or inspirational quotes.

5. Attach photos and words creatively in a collage on the vision board.

6. Display the vision board in an area of the home that is used daily.

7. Take time each day to contemplate the vision board and acknowledge any dreams or goals that have been accomplished.

A vision board alone will not attain these dreams or goals. It is simply an affirmation of what you want out of life. Viewing these dreams and goals daily will be a constant reminder of how life could be. It is up to you to be aware of what you want out of life, make the necessary changes, and take action to achieve these dreams and goals.

SYMBOLS, COLORS, SUPERSTITIONS, AND DREAMS

If a person believes in something or someone, those beliefs are truth for that person. Throughout history, cultures have looked for meaning or signs in everyday incidents. A visit from a cardinal or a butterfly is believed by some to be a visit from a deceased loved one. Breaking a mirror or opening an umbrella indoors is a sign of future bad luck. Do these incidents actually mean what people believe they mean? If it feels real for these people, it becomes their reality.

To learn more about signs found in daily experiences or nighttime dreams, look for answers in books or online. Anything—everyday items, the elements, the seasons, animals, colors, and so on—can be a symbol.

SYMBOLISM OF EVERYDAY ITEMS

* Wedding ring: Eternal love.

* Crown: Power or royalty.

* Horseshoe: Luck.

* Hourglass: Time.

With regard to the ancient elements, fire and air are described as masculine energies, while earth and water are feminine. This notion refers to the Hermetic principle of gender, discussed later in this book.

SYMBOLISM OF ANCIENT ELEMENTS AND SEASONS

* Fire: Destruction or rebirth.

* Air: Intelligence or breath of life.

* Water: Cleanliness or rejuvenation.

* Earth: Fertility or stability.

* Spring: Growth, birth.

* Summer: Heat, youth.

* Fall: Change, adulthood.

* Winter: Cold, death.

Other symbols found in nature include the four-leaf clover, which symbolizes luck. An egg or a tree is a symbol of life.

The sun and the moon have numerous meanings. According to Hermes Trismegistus' teachings, the sun is the father (masculine energy) and the moon is the mother (feminine energy). The sun can also symbolize knowledge, shedding light (day) on information. The moon can symbolize the mysterious, which is shrouded in darkness (night).

SYMBOLISM OF ANIMALS

* White dove: Love or peace.
* Lion: Courage.
* Dog: Companionship.
* Cat: Independence.
* Eagle: Freedom.
* Bear: Strength.
* Owl: Wisdom.

The list is a long one. If you interact with one of these symbols, you can take the experience as coincidence. However, the Hermetic principle of causation says that nothing happens by chance. So you can also reflect on the symbolism of the experience.

Colors have long been held to symbolize certain qualities and can affect mood.

SYMBOLISM OF COLORS

* Red: Anger, passion.

* Green: Envy, luck, new life.

* Purple: Royalty.

* Blue: Calm.

* Black: Power, evil.

* White: Purity, good.

* Yellow: Happiness.

If you want to find symbolism in your dreams, keep a dream journal near your bed and write down your dreams upon waking. Dreams are often fleeting, so a dream journal allows you to keep notes on specific events within the dream. You might find this approach to symbolism implausible, but the psychology of the subconscious has been an area of study for some time. In 1899 Sigmund Freud, neurologist and founder of psychoanalysis, published a book about the symbolism of dreams titled *The Interpretation of Dreams*. Freud's method was to ask the individual to interpret the possible symbolism of their own dreams based on the thoughts that came to mind when discussing different parts of the dream.

Currently, a more popular approach is consulting a dream dictionary, which lists hidden meanings of events that occur within dreams. These meanings vary, so take into consideration your own current affairs, emotions, and so on, to determine what your subconscious might be trying to communicate. Also examine the context of the dream. Review other events and actions in the dream to determine the meaning of each occurrence within the dream.

SYMBOLISM OF DREAMS

* Teeth: To lose teeth can relate to finances; to have a loose tooth can be a warning of untrustworthy friends; beautiful teeth can mean happiness.[60]

* Falling: To fall can symbolize fear and upcoming setbacks in life, but the outcomes can vary. For example, if the dreamer fell for a long time and was injured, the dreamer could face hardships for a significant period; if unhurt after the fall, the dreamer's setback will be brief.[61]

* Flying: To fly represents ambition, but other aspects of the dream play a role in the interpretation. For example, if the dreamer flew at a low or medium height, the goal will be achieved without much difficulty; straining to

---

60. Tom Corbett and Lady Stearn Robinson, *The Dreamer's Dictionary: From A to Z...3,000 Magical Mirrors to Reveal the Meaning of Your Dreams* (New York: Warner Books, 1994), 355.
61. Corbett and Robinson, *The Dreamer's Dictionary*, 146.

reach a higher altitude could foretell that the dreamer should change course to reach the goal.[62]

If you dream of a certain incident and find the meaning behind it, your analysis is not necessarily correct. Many variables must be analyzed before you can interpret a dream, including what you ate before going to bed, the state of your mental health before sleep, and outside noises or incidents that occurred during the night.

If you choose to believe in specific signs and symbols that you see around you or in your dreams, and these signs and symbols bring you joy, peace, insight, or a sense of calm, then accept them. Belief is in the mind of the beholder.

---

62. Corbett and Robinson, *The Dreamer's Dictionary*, 159.

Chapter 8

PRINCIPLE 2: THE PRINCIPLE OF CORRESPONDENCE

No problem can be solved from the same level of consciousness that created it.
—Albert Einstein, physicist

The notion that life is composed of different planes of existence may seem improbable. However, many believe in the existence of physical, mental, and spiritual well-being. These are planes of existence within the self. According to *The Kybalion*, the universe is divided into these three planes. A hard division among them may not be apparent, as each plane is part of the whole. The Hermetic principle of correspondence relates to these different planes: the material world, as well as the mental and spiritual planes.

As above, so below; as below, so above.
—The Kybalion

This principle, which speaks of subplanes of existence within planes of existence, can be a little more difficult to understand than the other six Hermetic principles. Although Hermes Trismegistus does not refer to a specific religion in his credited writings, the principle of correspondence can be found in The Lord's Prayer, which Jesus taught his disciples: "Thy kingdom come, Thy will be done in earth, as it is in heaven" (Matt. 6:10).

The Hermetic principle of mentalism says that what you think becomes your reality. So if negative, anxious, or impulsive thoughts are part of your everyday life, those thoughts become what you feel and discover in your experiences on the physical plane each day. But if you think positively or try to find the good in the bad, you more than likely have a better, more positive outlook on life and exude a more beneficial energy. The Hermetic principle of correspondence explains that whatever energy a person exudes will move into and return to that person in the physical realm.

For example, if your day starts with a stubbed toe, and you refuse to acknowledge and accept the incident and then move on, maybe you get stuck in a traffic jam on the way to work and get impatient. That impatience brews into anger. Once at work, the anger continues after you discover an error in the previous day's workload, creating additional turmoil. If you refuse to see that these occurrences are just the emotions of the moment and if you do not let go of the negativity to deal with the situation in an unemotional way, the negativity could continue. These unfortunate events began with a stubbed toe in the physical plane and continued in the physical plane because the mental plane could not accept, acknowledge, and move on from the initial unbeneficial thought and emotion. In this case, the principle is also working in accordance with the Hermetic principle of causation, or cause and effect, which is discussed later in this book.

But if you wake up, begin the day with self-affirmation or gratitude through meditation, prayer, or positive thoughts, and take unpleasant occurrences throughout the day in stride, always trying to stay aware of your emotions to correct any unbeneficial thoughts, the day will most likely be beneficial and fulfilling. Your mental state affects your physical state and vice versa.

This is also referred to as the law of attraction, which can be seen in many of the Hermetic principles, including mentalism, correspondence—the principle under discussion—and vibration. The way a day turns out is as you perceive it. If you change your perception by acknowledging your thoughts, then negative emotions and their physical effects can possibly be overturned. Once these feelings change, they can lead to more positive experiences.

Everything will not always be a good time or turn out the way you think it should. The Hermetic principle of rhythm, to be discussed later in this book, states that life is full of ups and downs. But if you can change your perception, then you can rise above the situation to a higher plane, thus having a more positive experience throughout your journey.

PLANES OF EXISTENCE AND BEYOND

To understand the Hermetic principle of correspondence, one can look at the recurring patterns in the natural world. For example, a spiral galaxy shape resembles the form of a hurricane. The nebula in space is similar to the design of the eye. The structure of the universe mirrors the synapses of neurons in the brain. The branches of a tree resemble its root system. The branches of a tree also look like the bronchial tree in the lungs. The river systems across the globe are comparable to the circulatory systems in the human body. "As above, so below; as within, so without."[63]

The Kybalion points out that within each plane, there are subplanes, and then there are subplanes within subplanes. Although there are various planes of existence, all planes come from the same source. *The Kybalion* states that all is part of THE ALL, and THE ALL exists within everything because everything is a creation of THE ALL. Each plane corresponds with the others because of this principle, and each plane is the same, just a varying degree of itself, as stated in the Hermetic principle of polarity, discussed later in this book. The physical plane is the lowest plane; the spiritual plane is the highest. If you are vibrating at a higher frequency, or if you are in a more positive state of being either through meditation, breathwork, practicing gratitude, and so on, then you can reach a higher plane, or a higher consciousness or higher self-awareness.

The Kybalion goes on to explain that within the spiritual plane exist unseen divinities and angelic helpers, which often intervene in physical and mental experiences. "Their occasional intervention and assistance in human affairs have led to the many legends, beliefs, religions and traditions of the race,

---

63. The Three Initiates, *The Kybalion*, 28.

past and present. They have super-imposed their knowledge and power upon the world, again and again, all under the Law of THE ALL, of course."[64] As part of THE ALL, these unseen divinities and angelic helpers were mortals and are described as "the advanced souls who have outstripped their brethren…in order to help the race on its upward journey along The Path."[65] It is said that only the most advanced Hermetists can grasp the powers of the spiritual plane. But everyone who yearns for knowledge can practice their way to enlightenment, or awareness, of themselves and the world around them.

WAYS TO SEEK ENLIGHTENMENT AND SELF-AWARENESS

Meditation and prayer can help guide those wishing to gain a higher consciousness to become more self-aware and learn to control their thoughts, emotions, and physical response. If you can reach a higher plane and continue to develop control over your emotions in order to "rise above" a situation, you will begin to let the negative pass below you. Attaining a higher level, or plane, of consciousness allows you, according

64. The Three Initiates, *The Kybalion*, 130.
65. The Three Initiates, *The Kybalion*, 131.

to *The Kybalion*, to "escape the swing of the Rhythmic pendulum (Principle of Rhythm) which [manifests] on the lower plane."[66] This law of neutralization consists of "the raising of the Ego above the vibrations of the Unconscious Plane of mental activity, so that the negative-swing of the pendulum is not manifested in consciousness, and therefore [a person is] not affected."[67] You can refuse to either participate in or deny the existence of something that could have a negative influence in your life. You can "rise above" or "take the high road" in circumstances that may not be beneficial.

It can take time to master this skill, but with practice comes great reward. Learning to calm the mind and focus on raising consciousness above the physical plane will ultimately lead a person to awareness and the true power within. Hermes Trismegistus' ancient texts say that God—otherwise known as the Good and the Father—created all, and within all is God energy. If a person can tap into God (the Source, the Creator) energy, which is already within, and come to the realization that everything and everyone is connected through this energy, there is no limit to what this individual can accomplish in this time and space.

---

66. The Three Initiates, *The Kybalion*, 163.
67. The Three Initiates, *The Kybalion*, 163.

MEDITATION

There are many styles and varieties of meditation, and benefits are associated with each. In the past few decades, the practice of meditation has become more mainstream, and more information is available to those wishing to learn this skill. Consider how you wish to benefit from meditation in choosing your path of self-discovery. In-person classes, held in a safe space, and online videos, viewed within the privacy of the home, can teach techniques ranging from basic to advanced meditation to those on the journey to enlightenment, or awareness, and peace.

The Hermetic principle of correspondence asserts that people can rise above negative energies, thoughts, and experiences and allow this negativity to pass beneath them, all while gaining a higher level of understanding and awareness. Charles A. Francis, author of *Mindfulness Meditation Made Simple: Your Guide to Finding True Inner Peace* and director of the Mindfulness Meditation Institute, began his journey into meditation with a group of a few friends in the 1990s. "I was intrigued," Francis shares. He later attended a retreat led by Zen master Thich Nhat Hanh. "It was more an experience of taking time to calm my mind, so I could see things better for myself." His meditation practice focused on one form of meditation at a time, including Buddhist Zen meditation, in which the meditator sits quietly and focuses on the breath. While practicing this type of meditation, Francis did not feel that he was learning what to do when his mind wandered. Buddhist meditation also focuses on being of service to others as a way to self-awareness. "I think that's helpful, but to me, the main vehicle for obtaining mindfulness, or enlightenment, is through meditation itself," Francis says.

Francis continued to educate himself about different meditation styles, such as Transcendental Meditation, which focuses on repeating mantras, and discovered mindfulness meditation, which is more secular. Francis describes himself as a practical, intellectual, and curious person, not religious, so mindfulness meditation was an ideal choice. Francis now shares his knowledge about mindfulness meditation techniques with others.

Mindfulness meditation stems from Buddhism, which teaches that you free yourself from suffering by allowing your mind to calm, thus enabling yourself to observe the world with more clarity. "Mindfulness meditation is the training of our mind that is designed to help us observe things as they really are, instead of our views being clouded by our emotions or our preconceived ideas," Francis states.

There are many benefits to this meditation, but the main one is helping practitioners deal with stress. "It lowers stress by calming the mind and calming our emotions," Francis explains. Thoughts trigger emotions, which can hinder a person from seeing things clearly. These emotions include fear of the unknown, impatience, anxiety, and so on. Mindfulness meditation helps calm the mind, so a person can view all sides of the reality of the situation.

Some mental health practitioners use mindfulness meditation to treat patients. It can help with depression, substance abuse, post-traumatic stress disorder, self-esteem, confidence, and so on. Learning to calm thoughts and emotions can also help improve relationships. People who practice meditation regularly may be less reactive when having a discussion with someone about personal or professional issues. Oftentimes disagreements arise from miscommunication or misunderstanding. "Very often, we don't finish listening to somebody's speech before we react. We often jump to a conclusion. We assume what they mean, and very often, it's totally different than what they actually mean," Francis explains. People often have difficulty expressing themselves—putting their thoughts and emotions into words—which can lead to misunderstanding. If you practice and create a habit of calming your own emotions, then you have a greater insight into what the other person is trying to express, and your response can be more appropriate to the situation.

Communication is key, and one simple statement can lead to a better understanding between parties. Oftentimes one person in a conversation is thinking of a response as the other person is talking, instead of actually listening and hearing what is being said. A technique for minimizing misunderstanding during a disagreement is to have one party share while the other party makes a conscious effort to listen. The conversation continues with the listener stating, "I heard you say____," summarizing the first party's statement. If the first party's statement is incorrectly understood, then the statement can be further explained. If the first party's statement is understood, then the second party can share, and so on, until the conversation leads to either agreement or an agreement to disagree. Both parties must keep an open mind but stick with their own truths.

This communication exercise can be used by parents and caretakers when dealing with adolescents. Parents and caretakers often tell children what to do or what not to do in order to teach them and keep them safe. But often a parent or caretaker may be busy and not give a young person their full attention when that person is trying to share. "Children need to be able to express themselves to somebody. Listening to them is a very important part of their development," Francis says. Through mindfulness meditation, a person can learn to calm the mind, which could create a habit of being able to focus and truly listen to others.

To truly learn how to calm thoughts and emotions can take years of practice. But once you practice mindfulness meditation for a short period of time, the benefits can be noticeable, such as feeling more relaxed. Practice will ultimately lead to developing a habit. If you embark on a meditation journey, keep in mind that other factors may affect the process, such as an overstimulated mind or background noise. But meditating for a few minutes during the day will make you more calm and less reactive. If you meditate for 10 to 20 minutes each day for two weeks, you can begin to observe improvements in your stress levels.

If you practice meditation for years, a stable mind becomes more the norm. Over time, the mind is reprogrammed. "You also become more insightful," Francis states. "What we gain from mindfulness meditation—we can see more cause and effect, the more things work together. We begin to understand ourselves better, how our mind works, how our body works, how our emotions work." Those who practice meditation become more aware of their triggers and can learn to be less reactive.

Concentrating during meditation develops the tool of observation. "We collect the facts, and we observe them, and we try to make sense of it objectively," Francis says. "We try not to let our previous views influence our judgment. By doing that, we see the world as it really is, and then we can make better decisions in our lives."

CONCENTRATE ON BREATH TO CALM THE MIND

1. Relax the body to set the tone. This encourages the mind to calm down.

2. Transition to concentration meditation. Follow your breathing by counting each breath, for example, 1 to 5. Stay focused on the breath to keep thoughts at bay. It is natural for the mind to wander. When it does, bring your focus back to the breath. Repeat counting breaths for several minutes.

3. Once the mind is settled, transition to mindfulness meditation. "We continue following our breathing but in a more relaxed way. We observe the overall breathing process instead of just one aspect of it," Francis explains.

4. When a stray thought appears, gently return to focusing on the breath. This calms the mind, provides insight, and trains the mind to observe, thus creating mental discipline.

"If we can't keep focused on anything, then how can we observe anything with any depth," Francis points out. Observations will remain superficial, and if the mind is distracted, you will not see beyond that distraction.

The practice of mindfulness meditation is simple. What can be difficult is sticking with it. "We're so easily distracted. When a greater priority happens in our life that we need to tend to, one of the first things we set aside is our meditation." Francis suggests that beginners immerse themselves in the practice: study meditation, join a meditation group, or both. This will help you get traction and continue the practice. The idea of mindfulness meditation is to rest the mind.

The practice of meditation can lead to enlightenment, or mindfulness, which is an awareness of what is happening within yourself and the world. "You begin to see how everything is interconnected. Nothing exists on its own," Francis shares. "As individuals, we all depend on the air that we breathe. We depend on the vegetation to produce the oxygen that we breathe," he continues. Most of the world's population depends on others to provide necessities, such as shelter, transportation, clothing, food, clean water, and so on. "We begin to appreciate it. It just gives us a much greater understanding, or it has for me, of how the whole world operates, the whole world works, the whole universe works, and that brings me a great deal of comfort."

Meditation can lead to emotional stability, less fear, and an improved memory. Physical health is an added benefit of this practice. Meditation can help reduce the risk of high blood pressure, heart disease, and other chronic illnesses. Mindfulness meditation can also boost the immune system. Research has found that mindfulness meditation preserves cells. "With cells, they are making copies of copies," Francis states. If it is a healthy cell, the cell that is reproduced will keep its integrity better than an unhealthy cell. "People become more aware of their mind and their body and how their actions and the things that they consume affect their body. They are more likely to live a healthier lifestyle, and therefore, reduce chronic illnesses," Francis explains. "It even slows the aging process."

For Francis, meditation is as important as eating healthy and exercising, and it has made his life more fulfilling. "It's good for you," he states. "You can choose not to do it. That's up to the individual. But it will just make your life so much better in just about every area."

THE POWER OF PRAYER

Prayer can calm a racing mind, give hope to a lost soul, and release worry in times of uncertainty. Prayer can lift you closer to the spirit. The principle of correspondence states that the universe includes many planes and subplanes of being, the lowest being grossest matter and the highest being the SPIRIT of THE ALL. These planes are separated only by a thin division. Every person should be searching for a path to their highest and greatest good, and meditation, contemplation, and attention to spirit can help them along the way. "[In] the degree that Man realizes the existence of the Indwelling Spirit [immanent] within his being, so will he rise in the spiritual scale of life. This is what spiritual development means—the recognition, realization, and manifestation of the Spirit within us."[68]

Prayer is a means to reach a higher spiritual connection. The physical, mental, and spiritual planes create the individual. Many times, the physical existence rules the individual

---

68. The Three Initiates, *The Kybalion*, 100.

because humans want to be satisfied, to be happy. Many attempt to achieve this satisfaction with physical gratification, which may not always meet their true needs. They search for a way to fulfill their needs through materialistic outlets, such as food, drugs, alcohol, and so on. "That then alters your mind, and puts your mind at rest, or at least numbs it, so that it's not screaming at you," Ryan Shearer, a believer of Jesus the Messiah, says. "The only true place to find absolute peace is going to be in the Spirit."

When it comes to prayer, sometimes a person may pray for a specific outcome or to fulfill a specific desire. "Sometimes we're praying for hopeful expectations. Sometimes we're praying for just presence of God," Shearer shares. One of Shearer's prayers was to witness God's work firsthand. His prayer was answered. During the fall of 2021, Shearer volunteered his services to help the pastor of his church, Real Family Fellowship, on a running ministry, The Heart of Elijah, through each of the 254 counties in the State of Texas in order to spread the word of God. Shearer planned to purchase a recreational vehicle to accompany his pastor during his run across the Lone Star State. Although he had mapped out his plan regarding when and how he would pay for and restore this RV, Shearer was about to receive a blessing and an answer to his prayer to witness God's work.

"The kingdom is amongst us and within us, yet no man can enter into the kingdom unless he's born of flesh and of the Spirit because the Spirit is what allows us to enter in," Shearer says. Shearer had been walking with the spirit for some time, and he had been praying for a firsthand glimpse of God's work. "And then you can start to see the fruits. Well, here comes this day of fruit."

Shearer was doing construction work for a local resident, and the two struck up a conversation. "We [began] talking about the Spirit, God's presence," he shares. They agreed that many lack the ability to recognize, realize, or live in the joy and peace that the spirit delivers. The conversation turned to the woman's recent stroke, which had led to the discovery of a blood clot in her brain. Doctors had told her that it was a miracle that she had not suffered previous symptoms. The stroke had left her basically unscathed other than a small loss of dexterity in her left hand. The conversation turned to Shearer's upcoming ministry, and he shared his plan to purchase the recreational vehicle to help transport his pastor. She asked him how much it would cost to start the ministry and explained that she had recently come into some money, and she and her family had been praying for a service to which to tithe the money. She then offered him the money to purchase the RV for the ministry. "I did get tears from just the whole thing," Shearer admits. "I mean, I'm asking for nothing, and yet God says, 'Here you go.'"

Shearer hesitated to take the donation at first. He asked if he could speak with her family. He called her son-in-law. "His response was, 'Well, praise God. That's awesome.' He said, 'We've been praying about this and who to give it to,'" Shearer explains.

The woman wrote Shearer a $10,000 check and said, "There's no strings attached. Do with it as you will. However, just know this, that it is God's money." Shearer admits it was definitely impactful. For him, the check was not even the greatest blessing. "It was just the fact that I was able to see God working in a way I've never seen before. And it was an answer to my prayer that, God, I want to be a witness of you working."

Many who are believers may still live in hopelessness. It is the individual's job to carry out the will of the spirit, "in earth, as it is in heaven," which refers to the principle of correspondence. God, the Source, the Creator, THE ALL, is willing to share the load if a person simply asks. "Once we receive the

Spirit that dwells and lives inside of us, it has given us eternal life," Shearer says.

When in prayer, you might not always know what to say, but it is an opportunity to return to the presence of the Spirit, God, THE ALL, the Creator, the Source. "And the presence is a gift," Shearer states. Many people are content as they are, but some may be curious about the power of prayer. Prayer does not always manifest as hoped for because it happens in accordance with the will of God, the Creator.

"Sometimes we're praying for the advancement of the kingdom, the advancement of God's will, for the betterment of other people," Shearer says. Prayers may or may not be answered, but blessings are apparent to many. A newly purchased vehicle can be attributed to God's blessing because He gave a person the ability to do the work to acquire the money to purchase it. To benefit from these blessings, you are required to live up to your potential, doing your part to make things happen.

HOW TO PRAY

1. Find a quiet place—or a chaotic one—at any time, day or night.

2. Think about your intention or start talking to God, a higher power, the Source, the Creator, THE ALL, aloud or in your thoughts.

3. Make a request or express thankfulness and appreciation.

4. Don't be afraid, feel ashamed, or feel stupid.

5. Repeat as needed.

"I'm still growing in my faith," Shearer shares. "We will always be growing in our faith and learning new things because that's just how it works."

Chapter 9

PRINCIPLE 3: THE PRINCIPLE OF VIBRATION

If you want to find the secrets of the universe, think in terms of energy, frequency, and vibration.
—Nikola Tesla, inventor and engineer

Everything, from the rocks and the air to the trees and the human race, is composed of energy and is in a constant state of vibration. It's science! Depending on the state of matter, the vibration varies. Atoms make up all matter, which is divided into four states—solid, liquid, gas, and plasma. Atoms in solids, such as wood, metal, minerals, and so on, are packed together tightly, so they have a lower vibration. If heat is added, the vibration increases. For example, heat added to an ice cube increases the vibration of the particles, and the ice melts into a liquid. If more heat is added, the vibration increases, and the liquid begins to evaporate, becoming a gas. If still more heat is added, it can cause the electrons to break away from the atoms to form plasma, which becomes electrically conductive. Examples of plasma include the stars and lightning.

Energy is everywhere. People feed off it. If someone is in an anxious or impatient mood (lower vibration), that person can affect the energy levels of those in the same room. An argument filled with anger can cause an abundance of negative emotions in one or both parties. But a hug from a loved one can have a calming effect, and a high five of congratulations can boost mood. Everyone can learn how to control their vibrations, or energy, to be more self-aware and to ultimately alter negative emotions into more positive or self-affirming feelings, thus attaining a higher vibration.

> *Nothing rests; everything moves;*
> *everything vibrates.*
> —The Kybalion

Energy forms, which include chemical, electrical, mechanical, and so on, are used and converted into different forms of energy. For example, the US Energy Information Administration (EIA) explains that humans eat food (chemical) to create energy, which is then used for mental and physical capacities (mechanical) or is converted into heat.

The EIA reports that energy cannot be created or destroyed. The law of conservation states that energy simply changes to another energy form, "but the total amount of energy in the universe stays the same."[69] *The Kybalion* states that the principle of vibration "embodies the truth that Motion [vibration or energy] is manifest in everything in the Universe"[70] and "THE UNIVERSE, AND ALL IT CONTAINS, IS A MENTAL CREATION OF THE ALL."[71] *The Kybalion* points out several times that nothing can exist outside THE ALL because THE ALL is infinite and "it must continuously exist forever, for there is nothing to destroy it, and it can never 'not-be,' even for a moment, because something can never become nothing."[72] All energy that exists within the universe, regardless of form, is connected and part of the whole. It may change form, such as a liquid evaporating into a gas, but energy never disappears.

If a wheel is turning slowly, humans can begin to hear a low-pitched sound, and as the wheel moves faster, the sound gets more high-pitched. The sound, or vibration, emitted

---

69. US Energy Information Administration, "What Is Energy? Laws of Energy," accessed June 29, 2021, https://www.eia.gov energyexplained/what-is-energy/laws-of-energy.php.
70. The Three Initiates, *The Kybalion*, 137.
71. The Three Initiates, *The Kybalion*, 70.
72. The Three Initiates, *The Kybalion*, 59–60.

because of the movement into the air waves, becomes higher and higher until the sound is no longer apparent, seeming to disappear into thin air. The sound energy did not disappear. The vibration continued to increase to higher levels until it appeared to no longer exist. The opposite is also true of low vibration. Rocks or other solid matter appear to be at rest because of their more static vibration.

VIBRATION IS ENERGY

The Hermetic principle of vibration is about energy. Energy is in everything—from the air that surrounds the earth and the tiny molecule to the sounds of the ocean and the heat of the sun. "Everything is a vibrational frequency. Due to the fact that everything is energy, it's all about frequency," states Jenny Parten, Reiki master and medicine woman. Once you understand that everything and everyone is in fact made of energy, it becomes easier to choose and focus on which vibrational frequency you emit. Vibrational frequency is a choice.

The principle of vibration works in tandem with the first Hermetic principle, the principle of mentalism. "Everything is a choice, and we often don't realize that. We think that life just unfolds before us, and then we just have to deal with the cards that are handed to us. It's not like that at all," Parten explains. You can control vibration by taking conscious actions and making conscious choices about what type of vibrational frequency you engage in and support. "If I'm staying stuck in these old patterns of behavior because I'm continuously playing over these old patterns in my mind, I'm constantly thinking about the past, I'm constantly focused on my trauma, I'm constantly thinking about the quote, unquote negative, [then] I'm bringing more of that energy into my experience all the time." Instead of focusing on the negative, work to change your mindset to focus more on the positive, or "the glass is half full," scenario. This will increase your vibration so that you express a more positive vibe.

Dealing with and overcoming trauma can be a difficult process, but with support from others, therapy, and a multitude of available self-help avenues, you can learn to overcome traumatic experiences. When choosing and accepting personal growth, you essentially show the universe what you want to experience more. Focusing on the positive instead of the negative will bring more positive occurrences into your life. "Energy flows where your attention goes," Parten states. "If I'm focused on this thing that I don't enjoy, that doesn't make me feel good, that's not what I want to experience more of, then I need to realize that I'm making choices that are not drawing me toward my highest and greatest good, that are not taking me toward that highest vibrational frequency." It takes work to learn and understand when you may need to refocus on the positive and change the energy you are emitting. Being conscious of your thoughts, conscious of your actions, and conscious of your reactions can help you refocus on the positive and vibrate at a higher frequency.

Creating healthy habits and being self-aware can help move your life journey toward growth. Becoming aware of which thoughts to focus on and which thoughts to recognize and release also helps you become more self-aware. Some thoughts may not be meant for your current time and space. "I'm not just grabbing onto every thought that comes into my head. So much thought is transient," Parten says. It can be difficult to learn which thoughts should be acted upon and which should be released. If you feel anxious in a situation that you cannot control, you might want to recognize this and make the conscious decision to breathe or use another method to release that anxiety, which will then change the frequency of your vibration, allowing you to take control of your emotions. In this way, you will increase your mental and physical well-being.

A person's energy vibrates at a higher frequency once the quality of that individual's spirit is healthier. It takes conscious effort, but you can raise your frequency by finding your true purpose. Everyone on this planet has a purpose. It could be to share information, to heal the sick, to create art, or something else. "If I don't know myself, I don't know what I love. If I don't know what I love, then I'm not going to be able to expand into the things that I am meant to expand in, in this time and space," Parten points out.

As discussed earlier, *The Kybalion* states that THE ALL, or THE UNKNOWABLE, God, the Creator, the Source, created everything and is in everything. Therefore your spirit is pure vibration and an authentic expression of yourself. The more you try to become self-aware and learn about yourself, the more you will learn the truth of your being. Once you are more aware of your truth, you will be able to connect more to THE ALL, or Pure Spirit. You will connect to the energy within that links humans with the Divine, or God energy. "The more that I realize that I'm also not just created by that energy but an expression of it, I am God energy manifest in human form, the more I also embody the quality of Creator. I realize the connectedness of everything, the value of everything, the unity, the oneness, the collective whole," Parten states. If humanity can come to an understanding that everyone and everything is connected, the human race can grow together and work together as a collective whole.

It is easy to say that change is needed, but for some it is not so easy to take action to create that change. Until you begin to make conscious choices and act to instigate a desired change, you will be stuck in a recurring cycle that may not be in your best interests. "When you get a little nudge that says, *Hey, you need to get up and move*, you get up and move. That is your soul space speaking to you," Parten explains. A person's soul space, intuition, God energy, is always talking and sharing information, but many times people push these thoughts away and focus on other things or make an excuse, such as, *I don't have time, I am afraid of the unknown*, or *It can wait*. Instead of putting off achieving your heart's desire or not moving toward fulfilling your life's purpose, you can begin to educate yourself and take more initiative toward discovering what you really want out of life.

WAYS TO HEAL ENERGY

Whether it is the simple act of focusing on the breath; learning energy work, such as Reiki; or spending time in nature, you can take control of your energy and move it toward a higher frequency, which will ultimately move you toward your true purpose, a higher consciousness, and the Divine.

Although everyone and everything is connected through energy, everyone has a different quality of energy, a different vibratory frequency. God energy is an aspect of everyone's being, but it is being filtered through humanity, which includes life experiences, emotions, and so on. "It's almost like you have this big light that is Source energy, and it's filtering itself through all these amazing different crystals. The light that is going to manifest from each crystal is going to be completely different because each crystal is a different color, it's a different shape, totally different from one from the other. No two are the same," Parten explains. Each crystal manifests its own miraculous light, which is necessary to inspire hope and uplift others. Once you decide to become more aware of your emotions and your energy, you can implement techniques and tools to vibrate at a higher frequency and embody a more positive energy, thus emitting it beyond yourself.

"We're all healers," Parten shares. "We are meant to do our own healing work. Sometimes we need somebody to hold our hand and walk through it with us, through the dark space, or hold a safe space for us, so we can do certain things.

Sometimes trauma is deep. Sometimes things are very challenging." Asking for help and using resources along the way will empower you to work with your own energy and heal it. Investing in the energy that you would like to embody—through meditation, exercise, time spent in nature, and so on—and learning how to emit a higher vibratory frequency are powerful tools. *The Kybalion* states that, with proper instruction and practice, humanity can create vibrations at will through the art of Hermetics. "He who understands the Principle of Vibration has grasped the sceptre of Power."[73]

NUTRITION: GOOD FOR THE BODY, MIND, EMOTIONS, AND SPIRIT

The food you consume creates energy for your body. With so many fad diets and eating trends today, it might be difficult to know what will work best for you. The most important aspect of eating habits is sustainability. Many times, people start a diet or a healthier way of eating, and then the new diet goes by the wayside. Maybe these individuals believe they do not have the time to prepare healthy foods, the cost becomes unmanageable, or they lose their willpower. All

---

73. The Three Initiates, *The Kybalion*, 147.

these and any other reasons refer back to the Hermetic principle of mentalism. If you believe it can be done, then it can.

Finding what works regarding nutrition and healthy eating is key. It is about trial and error. If the Atkins diet or the Paleolithic diet did not work, there are plenty of other healthy eating plans available. The information is out there. Nutritionists can customize eating plans based on a person's needs or desires. Regardless of the avenue to healthy eating, nutrition is beneficial to physical, mental, emotional, and spiritual well-being. Find something that works and stick with it.

The most common healthy eating plan is to eat small portions of healthy foods several times throughout the day. These frequent small meals boost metabolism for a longer period. Some nutritionists say eating "good carbs," such as whole wheat bread or oatmeal, earlier in the day instead of late at night, can be beneficial. Cutting back on highly processed foods—including frozen dinners, fast foods, fried foods, and sodas—and minimizing saturated fats can also promote a healthier lifestyle. Eating lean proteins, such as chicken, specific fruits and vegetables such as leafy greens, certain carbs, and healthy fats, for example avocadoes and nuts, can mean a more advantageous physical, mental, emotional, and spiritual existence.

The Hermetic principle of correspondence ("As above, so below; as below, so above") can also be seen in the principle of vibration with regard to how certain foods provide nourishment (and energy) to specific parts of the body. For example, a walnut, which resembles the brain, is said to be beneficial to brain health. Tomatoes, when cut in half, resemble the heart. Tomatoes have many health benefits, including reducing the risk of heart disease. Ginger root resembles the stomach and reportedly aids digestion. When chopped, the inside of a carrot looks like the iris and pupil of the eye. Due to their beta-carotene, carrots have health benefits for the eye.

Healthy foods provide the vitamins and minerals needed to sustain the body. Certain foods boost chemicals in the body that affect physical, mental, and emotional well-being. For example, the potassium in bananas helps with muscle recovery. Zinc in oysters reportedly benefits the sex drive. And the antioxidants in dark chocolate are good for heart health. The benefits that vitamins and minerals provide are numerous.

Staying hydrated helps flush toxins from the body and replenish the body's fluids, so water should be your go-to drink. Healthy foods, when eaten correctly, can naturally boost your mood and increase your metabolism. The main takeaway about healthful eating is to eat more natural foods and drink more water, both of which God put on this earth. A nutritious diet provides a multitude of benefits and helps increase energy, which can lead to a higher vibratory frequency, which, according to Hermes Trismegistus' teachings, is an important life goal.

BREATHWORK CAN CALM, OPEN ENERGIES

The breath can calm the body as well as the mind. A parent may tell an inconsolable child to take a deep breath in hopes of calming the tantrum. Counting to 10 as you breathe can stabilize an angry mood. These breath techniques to calm or control energies have been passed down from generation to generation. The breath can bring your attention back to yourself, allowing you to refocus on the reality of a situation instead of your emotions about or misperceptions of your experience.

A popular breathing technique is to take a series of slow, deep breaths. This lets you center yourself, and it stabilizes your mood. When breathing out, expel the breath as completely as possible, and then inhale in a way that the breath seems to push out the stomach. This method allows the lungs to take in more oxygen compared with shallow breathing.

Another breathwork technique making its way through schools and the corporate world is the four-square breathing technique, or the box breathing technique. This simple technique gives you a chance to refocus your mind, calm your energy, and take control of your emotions.

TAKE TIME TO BREATHE: FOUR-SQUARE, OR BOX, BREATHING

1. Find a comfortable seat. Sit upright with your back straight, and gently roll your shoulders back and down.

2. Exhale deeply. Slowly breathe in through the nose for four seconds.

3. Hold the breath for four seconds.

4. Slowly release the breath for four seconds.

5. Hold for four seconds.

6. Continue the breathing technique as needed.

7. For a visual aide, use your forefinger to draw the top of the box in the air in front of you on the four-second inhalation. Move the forefinger down to draw one side during the four-second breath hold. Draw the bottom of the box on the four-second exhale. Finally, draw the other side of the box during the final four-second hold.

You can use different breathwork modalities to achieve your desired results. Kundalini yoga employs breathwork, mantras (phrases or sounds repeated during meditation), and specific postures to awaken energy in the body. Kundalini yoga started in ancient India and made its way to the West in the late 1960s. The practice focuses on opening energies that move from the base of the spine (the root chakra) to the top of the head (the crown chakra). Along the way, these energies are opened, allowing them to flow freely and create balance.

In-person classes and online classes and videos are available for those wanting to learn more about kundalini yoga. A class may begin with a mantra to tune into the practice and continue with kriyas, or specific postures or movements, which are paired with lengthy breath exercises. Throughout the class, you can build and balance energies, focus that energy on certain areas of concern within your body, and ultimately reach a higher clarity of mind and spirit. The class usually closes with meditation and a mantra. Learning to build and control your energy through breathwork and kundalini yoga can lead to physical, mental, emotional, and spiritual benefits.

VIBRATIONAL HEALING

The practice of using vibration to heal has been around for thousands of years. Vibrational healing could incorporate energy work, such as Reiki, or it could incorporate sound as a means to heal.

Reiki, or energy healing, is a practice from Japan. The practitioner is a conduit who funnels outside energy to the receiver. Often hovering the hands over the client's body, the practitioner works to channel energy to the receiver in hopes of helping the client heal physical, mental, or emotional discomfort.

Sound vibrations have long been used as a healing method. Incorporate sound vibrational healing into your own practice with gongs, tuning forks, or singing bowls. Every instrument is attuned to a specific frequency, and by using this frequency, you can attune yourself to its vibration. Different sound frequencies (hertz of different pitches) have been found to have healing qualities. The research continues.

SPEND TIME WITH NATURE

The simple act of stepping outside on a sunny day for a breath of fresh air or taking advantage of the shade of a mature oak tree can improve one's attitude and outlook. Whether the cause is breathing in the oxygen the plants expel, feeling gratitude for the beauty of nature with her vibrant colors in different hues, smelling the fragrance of flowers or recent rains or freshly cut grass, or replenishing vitamin D through sunlight, nature can provide a multitude of health and well-being benefits, physically, mentally, emotionally, and spiritually.

Charlie Hall, PhD, professor at Texas A&M University, Department of Horticultural Sciences, and holder of the Ellison Chair in International Floriculture, says the number one benefit to experiencing nature is that it reduces cortisol levels, which in turn reduces stress. This reduction in stress due to the influence of the natural world is available to those of all ages. If plants or flowers are displayed in a classroom or if students have a view of nature, they have been found to perform better on standardized tests and daily assignments. Plants or flowers are often delivered to sick patients to boost their moods. And in a 1984 study, Roger S. Ulrich, PhD, discovered that a view of nature in a hospital room means patients recover more quickly and require less pain medication.[74]

Nature is also beneficial to elderly individuals, particularly those with dementia or Alzheimer's disease. "There's a tremendous benefit in terms of their memory retention, both short term and long term, if [family members or staff members] can get them outside or experiencing nature within their rooms," Hall states. Hall, who grew up in the nursery industry, recalled opportunities when he implemented nature while visiting his father, who passed away from dementia. "Anytime we could get Dad outside just potting up a plant," he shares, "and get his hands in the dirt, it was like old Dad again."

Many Alzheimer's disease clinics have healing gardens, which benefit not only the patients but also the staff. When staff members see plants and flowers in the workplace, it reduces stress, employee turnover, absenteeism, and pre-

74. Roger S. Ulrich, "View from a Window May Influence Recovery from Surgery," *Science* 224, no. 4647 (1984): 420–21, https://www.jstor.org/stable/1692984.

senteeism, which means working while not fully engaged. "Anytime you can surround yourself with nature, both outside and in the built environment, it has those benefits," Hall explains.

Biophilic design incorporates nature in the architecture of living and working spaces. "That's incorporating a lot of natural lighting through sky lighting. It's incorporating water in both [the] aspects of hearing water and seeing water and fountains," Hall says. "Most of the research has shown that when you're outside, particularly from a physiological standpoint, it just has a lot of benefits." Regardless of whether people view nature indoors or outdoors, it has a positive effect. "We're creatures of light anyway, so we prefer being in a sunny setting versus dark and dreary."

Gardening has added benefits. "If you're active outside, gardening or landscaping, it's a double whammy because it's good exercise, and of course you are in that environment where, as my mom used to say, 'The molecules orbit differently,'" Hall shares. "You get your hands in the dirt, then there's mycorrhizae and certain micro-elements in the dirt that are beneficial as well. It is one of the better ways to enhance your immune system to just get your hands dirty," Hall states. There is also the benefit of edibles gardening.

"You get to see the fruit of your labor." Gardening can also build self-esteem, satisfaction, and a better understanding of the circle of life when disease or weather destroys the plants.

School gardens are a tremendous benefit to children and teenagers. "When they're getting their hands dirty like that, they're not so concerned about what each other is wearing or what shoes they have on or the color of their skin. So it's kind of a great equalizer from a socialization standpoint of those kids. It's pretty remarkable," Hall shares. "When kids have a hand in growing the vegetables, they eat them." The students can then take that enthusiasm for fruits and vegetables home. Research shows that parents begin to eat healthier because the children want to make healthier eating decisions.

Horticultural programs implemented in prisons have also benefited inmates. The rates of recidivism, or reoffending after release, drop dramatically for inmates who spend time outside gardening. "Maybe they've experienced that nurturing aspect. Maybe it's a positive experience for them growing their own food [or that] they've developed a horticultural skill," Hall explains. The Junior Master Gardener Program was first implemented in a women's prison in Bryan, Texas, just outside College Station, where Texas

A&M University is located. The children who were visiting their mothers spent time gardening, and now the program is international. This program has benefits for everyone involved.

Adding parks, community gardens, and landscaping to abandoned urban areas has helped cut crime, including violent crime. The introduction of nature to inner cities not only provides fresh fruits and vegetables for consumption, but also adds beauty, puts more eyes on the streets, and increases intergenerational involvement in civic life. Horticultural programs are also therapeutic for the population with physical or mental disabilities. Planting seeds benefits mental health, making these gardeners more prone to peaceful behavior; increases memory; and can help with fine motor skills. "That alone helps them to eat and do other things in their normal lives," Hall shares, "and it helps build that muscle dexterity that's critically important to them."

The power of plants to heal body, mind, emotions, and spirit could be attributed to many things. "I think the added oxygen has something to do with that and their ability to scrub particulates and volatile organic compounds out of the air," Hall theorizes. Or it could be the beauty of nature, which can cause one to feel grateful, thus increasing the person's energy frequency.

Even if you don't have the opportunity to spend much time outdoors, you can always bring live plants into your home or office. Some people may not have a green thumb, but Hall reminds everyone not to worry about killing the plants and to enjoy them while they are alive. "It's just a part of it. It's the cycle of life. A plant, a succulent, or an orchid, or whatever, is not meant to live forever." And if the plant's life cycle is cut short, you can always plant more.

Nature is not just about plants, flowers, trees, and shrubs. The natural world is so much more. Spending time outdoors hiking, biking, floating the river, riding horses, watching birds eat from a feeder, or walking the dog will boost energy levels and mood either through the fresh air, the gratitude you feel while taking in the sunlight, or simply the experience of Mother Nature.

TAKEAWAYS

1. Spend time outdoors every day (wear sunscreen or dress in lightweight long-sleeve shirts and trousers).

2. Add plants and flowers indoors; let in the light.

3. Enjoy what Mother Nature provides.

4. Plant a garden.

5. Take time to smell the roses.

Chapter 10

PRINCIPLE 4: THE PRINCIPLE OF POLARITY

People desire to separate their worlds into polarities of dark and light, ugly and beautiful, good and evil, right and wrong, inside and outside. Polarities serve us in our learning and growth, but as souls we are all.

—Joy Page, actress

When you have a fever, you might shiver as if you were cold. You might be so happy that you shed tears, as if you were feeling sad. Or you might be so angry that you begin to feel a calmness encompass your being. These are several examples of how a person can experience the principle of polarity—the dual poles, the exact opposites—in physical and emotional experiences.

The Hermetic principle of polarity states that everything has an opposite, but it's just a different degree of the same thing. Darkness is the absence of light, cold is the absence of heat, and so on. There is no absolute within the principle of polarity, just varying degrees. It is all relative.

Everything is Dual; everything has poles; everything has its pair of opposites; like and unlike are the same; opposites are identical in nature, but different in degree; extremes meet; all truths are but half-truths; all paradoxes may be reconciled.
—The Kybalion

This principle states that opposites are the same, just various degrees of the extremes, so there is no way to determine when one thing truly becomes the opposite. For example, "What is the difference between 'Large and Small'? Between 'Hard and Soft'? Between 'Black and White'? Between 'Sharp and Dull'? Between 'Noise and Quiet'? Between 'High and Low'? Between Positive and Negative'"?[75] These various degrees of opposites are based on perception. A childhood bedroom may feel spacious to a five-year-old, but as an adult, the room becomes smaller than in that individual's memories. A person who is hard of hearing may need to increase the

---

75. The Three Initiates, *The Kybalion*, 33–34.

volume of the television despite the fact that others say the volume is too loud.

Another example of the principle of polarity is love and hate. There are degrees of like and dislike within these two opposites, just as there are degrees of love and hate. The Hermetists believed it is possible to change hate to love or change evil to good by using the will to change the vibration, thus transmuting the lower, more negative opposite to a higher, more positive vibration. They called this the art of polarization or mental alchemy. The transmutation would not change something into a different thing—for example, it would not change heat to fear—but it would change the degree of opposites, ultimately benefiting a person's mental state.

POLARITY: A PARADOX

The principle of polarity results in the divine paradox, or the paradox of the universe. A paradox is contradictory but in the end is truth. *The Kybalion* states, "The truly wise, knowing the nature of the Universe, use Law against laws; the higher against the lower; and by the Art of Alchemy transmute that which is undesirable into that which is worthy, and thus triumph."[76] The Three Initiates write, "Transmutation, not presumptuous denial, is the weapon of the Master."[77] In other words, change is necessary if you want to grow, learn, and live at your highest vibration, ultimately growing closer to THE ALL, God, the Source.

The divine paradox of absolute and relative may be difficult to grasp because it is informed by the principle of polarity. All truths are but half-truths. There are two sides to every story, two points of view. "Absolute Truth has been defined as 'Things as the mind of God knows them,' while Relative Truth is 'Things as the highest reason of Man understands them.'"[78] To a human's finite mind, the universe is real and humans are subject to natural law: fire burns, gravity is a force, and so on. Humans also recognize that although matter exists—from a piece of paper to the human body—all matter is simply atoms vibrating at varying rates of speed.

The principle of polarity works in conjunction with the other Hermetic principles, including the principle of vibration. For example, "Spirit and Matter are but the two poles of the same thing, the intermediate planes being merely

---

76. The Three Initiates, *The Kybalion*, 77.
77. The Three Initiates, *The Kybalion*, 77.
78. The Three Initiates, *The Kybalion*, 82.

degrees of vibration."[79] On the musical scale, the higher the note, the higher the vibration. Temperature increases as the vibration increases. The higher the vibration of any matter, or energy—the closer to the more positive side of the pole—the closer it is to THE ALL, the Source, God, the Creator.

The Kybalion encourages readers to seek an understanding of mental laws and the nature of the universe and use this understanding to progress through life. According to Hermetic philosophy, all of creation comes from the mind of and exists within THE ALL. This is why we are instructed, "do not feel insecure or afraid" and "rest calm and secure."[80]Although nothing in existence will ever actually become THE ALL or the Creator, the Creator exists within everything. "While All is in THE ALL, it is equally true that THE ALL is in All. To him who truly understands this truth hath come great knowledge."[81]

The principle of polarity teaches that, with awareness and recognition, opposites can be reconciled. Things can never become different: hot will never become fear, cold will never become sharp, and so on. Neither opposite is an absolute,

---

79. The Three Initiates, *The Kybalion*, 150.

80. The Three Initiates, *The Kybalion*, 85.

81. The Three Initiates, *The Kybalion*, 95.

but it can be transmuted, or changed, into a higher degree, thus benefiting a person's mental state.

RECOGNIZING AND APPLYING POLARITY

To take advantage of the Hermetic principle of polarity, one must first recognize it as law: each pair of opposites is a varying degree of the same thing. From there, a person can raise awareness of these opposites in everyday life and make conscious, more mindful decisions to deal with what is presented in each life experience. For example, if overwhelmed with fear, a person might want to focus on how to lessen that fear and move to the positive side of the pole of opposites by developing courage.

You can learn to be more in control of your thoughts and emotions in many ways, from therapy and mindfulness to meditating with crystals (see page 124 for more information on working with crystals). It takes effort, awareness, and work to tip the scales in your favor, but in time it can be accomplished. It will not always be easy, but understanding the principle of polarity and how to deal with it skillfully could lead to a happier and healthier life, physically, mentally, emotionally, and spiritually.

THERAPEUTIC SUPPORT

You might think that finding balance or neutrality between the poles related to the principle of polarity is the ultimate goal. But there is more to life than finding balance between opposites. Instead, try to attain a more positive degree of the opposites. Focus on changing your mentality to a healthier state. This could benefit your physical, mental, emotional, and spiritual well-being.

"It's not enough to just reduce negative emotions or manage negative emotions. You have to improve and increase positive emotions," says Jennifer Kim Penberthy, PhD, ABPP, board certified licensed clinical psychologist, Chester F. Carlson Professor of Psychiatry and Neurobehavioral Sciences at the University of Virginia School of Medicine. "We don't want you to just survive. We want you to thrive. Mental health is thriving," she explains. If you can learn to intentionally develop positive emotions, this will promote and increase your overall well-being.

If you feel neutral—which is not really good or bad but a degree in the middle of these two poles—you could begin to change this neutral feeling to a more pleasant, positive feeling through mindfulness practice. Penberthy suggests focusing on thoughts of gratitude, which will improve mood. "We can change emotions, and many times, people will push back and say, 'Well, no, that's ridiculous. I can't help the way I feel. I just feel it.'" She responds to her patients by questioning them about whether they can make themselves feel worse. "Almost everyone says, 'Oh, of course I can make myself feel worse.'" If people can create a reality in which they feel worse, they can also create a reality in which they feel better. Adapt your thinking and you can manage your emotions.

It is a difficult process and takes work, but with practice, consciously changing your negative emotions can become habit. "The beginning point is you have to have motivation to do so and think it's important," Penberthy says. Emotional change is easier if you focus on your values. "I would love to see more people in general working on positive values and qualities," Penberthy shares. Consciously implementing your values in your daily life can help you cultivate positive emotions and behavioral choices. Penberthy suggests developing a mission statement, which identifies your purpose and your goal in every aspect of your life, including partner-ships, raising children, and employment. "That really helps people orient themselves and focus on the values they want to embody and want to live."

For example, if you are angry and want to lash out, you could instead turn your attention to your mission statement and think, *What would someone with this value choose to do in this situation?* "What would the fair person do? What would the honest person do? What would the loyal person do?" Penberthy asks. She suggests practicing a specific value each month. "I think about what would the world look like if we could all do that and how would our mental health, quality of life, our well-being be improved if we could do that on purpose," she says.

Everyone is born with basic emotions, such as fear, disgust, joy, and anger. Some emotions, such as fear, can be viewed as negative. But fear can be a good thing. For example, when an experience sparks fear, the fight, flight, or freeze response is triggered. If a threat is imminent, fear can motivate a person to flee the scene to safety.

Other fears may not be as beneficial. "Is it really that scary? Am I making things up? Am I having anxious thoughts about things that haven't happened?" Penberthy questions. She suggests using a combination of cognitive, behavioral, and mindfulness therapies to help yourself regulate emotion in the moment. You can also reach out to a professional or educate yourself on techniques and skills to improve mental health.

Oftentimes you might realize that you're depressed or anxious. If depression or anxiety is strong, acknowledge it, take a deep breath, and refocus. These conscious actions can help reduce depression or anxiety and improve your mood. But if you're depressed or anxious, you might not recognize it. Others might be more aware of it than you are. "It's important to have people around you that you can trust that can help assess how you're doing," Penberthy says.

Some people have a malicious intent when pointing out another person's mental health issues. They project their own possible mental health issues into the situation. This can be a challenge for the person who receives this information. "It's important to be more aware of your own state of being, who you feel comfortable trusting, and who you think knows you," Penberthy states. "Knowing boundaries and recognizing what is mine to own, my emotions, my behaviors, my thoughts, my feelings, and then what is another person's that they need to own. That's on them."

Mental health issues are related to biology, psychology, and sociology. "It's really important to know and think about the environment we were raised in. Did we have adverse childhood experiences? What did we learn from the people that raised us? What were our experiences in our culture?" Penberthy says all of these experiences can influence mental health. Genetics (biological) can be exacerbated by environment through parenting. The parent may have been abused or never been shown love, so these issues could be transferred to the child. "As the child gets older and has more autonomy over their life, we often have to go back and help them realize, okay, you had no choice but to be in that environment when you were younger and to accept that this was the reality. Now, you can see and demarcate that your parents' stuff is their stuff. It's not yours, and you don't have to take responsibility for it anymore," Penberthy says. "You don't have to believe what they say if they are saying you are worthless. You don't have to believe that. You can look at yourself and judge for yourself what you've achieved, what you base worth on." Recognizing boundaries helps promote sustainable mental health and wellness.

Regarding trauma, which can foster poor mental health, Penberthy says the past cannot be erased or undone, but it can be a learning experience. She likened dealing with trauma to updating a computer program. "You were programmed early on to believe certain things or to feel certain things, and you were programmed by someone who was broken," Penberthy explains. "We're going to build on that, and we're going to create healthier learning now." You can use strategies to build positive experiences in your present reality. Use mindfulness to check in with yourself and reflect on how your mental health status, quality of life, and stress level could be affecting your life experiences. Using techniques such as understanding and labeling the emotion, and reaching out to a professional or other trusted person to discuss the issue could help you sort through the situation.

TAKEAWAYS

1. Use mindfulness to evaluate yourself and determine what emotion you are feeling.

2. Recognize the degree of your emotion and its effect on your mental state; label it.

3. Focus on your values or your mission statement to change your emotion to a more positive mental state.

4. Set boundaries; accept responsibility for your own mental state but not the mental state of others.

5. Ask for support from a professional or another person you trust.

THE HEALING ENERGY OF CRYSTALS

Using crystals for healing might seem unrealistic, but this method has been used for thousands of years. For those who believe in the power of crystals, these "rocks" can provide a constant healing vibration.

Summer Darvischi, who owns Open Hearts Yoga Sanctuary and Open Hearts Crystal Blessings in Granbury, Texas, has been working with crystals for nearly a decade. Her journey began after exhausting every avenue within the health industry to heal her physical and emotional issues. After advocating for her health and working with doctors, specialists, and therapists, she found that nothing was helping her heal. Darvischi began a holistic healing journey in hopes of discovering a way to feel better. "I became an avid student of all things crystals." At the time, Darvischi taught math and science at a Christian school. "The metaphysics of the geology of the crystals really was what convinced me to go on a different path because I had enough science background to understand the metaphysics of how things worked." She immediately began to feel better emotionally once she started working with crystals. "There was something to it."

Darvischi began taking classes and reading books about crystals and energy healing. "I became a constant student and practitioner," she explains. She had already delved into meditation, and after experimenting with crystals and improving her mental and emotional health, she wanted to focus more on physical movement and began yoga classes. She was drawn to teach others what she had learned about the healing power of crystals, meditation, and yoga, so she opened her own wellness center. "If other people can find healing in my healing journey, I want to make that accessible to them."

According to both science and the Hermetic principle of vibration, everything has a measurable vibration. "A crystal has a solid, static, stable vibration, and humans do not," Darvischi states. "God, Source, Spirit, Creator—whatever you want to call it—puts things on this planet for us for the purpose of healing, like essential oils, and plants, and rocks, and trees," she explains. "All of these things are here for the human world to have available for holistic healing."

A crystal's healing vibration never wavers. But a person's vibrational frequency can change with thoughts and emotions, and these thoughts and emotions can lead to anxiety, depression, impatience, and so on. "A crystal can bring us into a more static, steady, solid healing vibration. So, scientifically, it's kind of like acoustics. The loudest amplitude wins." Everything will come into resonance with the loudest, or strongest, vibration, which can be found in crystals. This could ultimately change a person's vibration to a higher state and increase the person's mood to a more positive side of the pole of opposites.

For example, you attend a party you were reluctant to go to because you had been having a bad day or just had been in a miserable mood. Everybody at the party is dancing and having a great time. "You will likely be pulled out of that funk that you might have been in before that and said, 'I'm not going to have a good time.' When you walk into a room with thirty people in it that are obviously happy to see you and having a good time, that will pull you into a higher vibration," Darvischi says. The same can happen with negative emotions. For example, if you arrive home from work and find that everyone in the house has been arguing, those individuals may exude a heavy, negative energy. If you are not in balance, with a strong, high vibration, you could get pulled into the stress and energy of this situation. Working with healing crystals and learning to manage energies can help you be more aware and cognizant of how to control your own emotions when you encounter negative energetic situations.

Because of its stable vibration, a crystal can have physical and emotional healing qualities. People who use crystals can receive their energy, which benefits their own energetic vibration.

* Carnelian: For physical vitality and healing; to boost energy.
* Blue calcite: For relaxation.
* Lepidolite: To calm anxiety.
* Rose quartz: For unconditional love and heart healing.

There are many ways to use crystals, including during meditation. In meditation, you calm the mind to gain distance from your emotions, think more clearly, and hear your intuition so you can separate fact from emotion. "When you add a crystal into that, and you become a crystal meditator, you can really get in tune with these vibrations and what the universe has to say to you or what Mother Earth has to say to you through the jewels that came from her belly," Darvischi explains.

Intuition can guide you to place the crystal on certain parts of your body, depending on what you want to accomplish, such as healing a certain part of the body or clearing a blocked chakra. Some people put the crystal on the heart, the belly, or the forehead. When teaching, Darvischi typically asks her students to hold the crystal in their left hand. "That is the receptive, or the yin, side of the body," she explains. "When we open up the receiving hand, place the crystal in the hand, and allow ourselves to be open to receive, we are able to receive those vibrations quite powerfully."

Crystal grids can also be used to amplify and utilize energy. "One of the greatest things about crystal grids is that we cannot, as humans, maintain our focus all the time, but the more focus that we can develop, obviously the faster our goals and intentions are going to manifest and form. The crystal grid holds that space for us all the time because it has that static, stable frequency, and it has the ability to hold information and hold space." Darvischi explains that quartz crystals are especially beneficial when used in a crystal grid. Quartz is often used in computers, smartphones, and laptops to store memory and battery power.

When you think back to childhood, you may remember exploring the yard and picking up rocks to put in your pockets, giving pebbles to your parents as tokens of appreciation, or even having a pet rock. "We know that innately, that when we put a rock in our pocket, we feel better," says Darvischi. There are differences between rocks and crystals based on composition and form. But to some, both can have healing qualities. It may not be something that is profound, but these small pieces of nature, specifically crystals, can soothe vibration, bringing a person back to the positive side of the pole of opposites.

TAKEAWAYS

1. Crystals have a solid, stable vibration; they can be used to balance or amplify energies.

2. Research crystals and identify which ones to use for your desired outcome.

3. Find a class or group to move forward with your crystal journey.

4. Meditate on intentions, placing crystals on specific parts of your body or holding them in your left hand.

5. Be open to receive.

Chapter 11

PRINCIPLE 5: THE PRINCIPLE OF RHYTHM

Life is like a roller coaster. Ups, downs, twists, and turns, but what a ride!
—Lisa Layden, thought leader

Life has its ups and downs, its highs and lows. According to the credited writings of Hermes Trismegistus, this roller coaster called life follows a law: the principle of rhythm. The third principle, the principle of vibration, states that everything is in a constant state of vibration, while the fourth principle, the principle of polarity, discusses how everything is a varying degree of opposites. And the fifth principle, the principle of rhythm, takes these laws into greater depth, stating that life is like a pendulum, and once it moves one way, it must return to the opposite side.

During the late 1600s, when several theologians and researchers began translating Trismegistus' written works, Sir Isaac Newton became known for the discovery of gravity. One quote attributed to Newton, "What goes up must come down," is a description of the effect gravity has on objects. Newton's law of universal gravitation proves that the principle of rhythm has scientific merit.

> *Everything flows, out and in; everything has its tides; all things rise and fall; the pendulum-swing manifests in everything; the measure of the swing to the right is the measure of the swing to the left; rhythm compensates.*
> —The Kybalion

According to Newton's third law of action and reaction, for every action or force in nature there is an equal and opposite reaction. According to *The Kybalion*, the principle of rhythm gives reason to the ebb and flow of the ocean waves, which are always moving inward and outward. If a negative event occurs, a positive event will also occur to balance the scales. *The Kybalion* calls it the law of compensation, which is considered a universal law. Can you understand true pleasure if you haven't experienced pain or challenges? Emotions and feelings are always changing, rising and falling. You might feel fear before starting a new job or speaking in public. But a boost of courage will overtake you once you begin to feel more confident in your abilities.

With life, death is inevitable. Night always follows day, and seasons continue their cycles as each year advances. People will move in and out of your life, but they always appear for a reason: to teach, inspire, guide, support, and so on. Life will always have ups and downs, but you can learn to rise to a higher plane to escape the swing of the pendulum, which is evident in the Hermetic principle of rhythm. *The Kybalion* labels "rising above" as the law of neutralization. If you can raise your awareness and your vibration, then you can allow the unnecessary turbulence of a situation to pass below you. This allows you to take control and take conscious steps to refuse to participate in the backward negative swing of the pendulum, which is apparent in the principle of rhythm.

You can't have your cake and eat it too: this expression refers to the law of rhythm. You cannot keep the cake in your possession if you choose to eat it. As stated in *The Kybalion*, "No one can 'keep his penny and have the bit of cake' at the same time."[82] You won't have the penny you used to purchase the piece of cake once the payment has been made. *The Kybalion*

---

82. The Three Initiates, *The Kybalion*, 169.

goes on to state, "The things that one gains are always paid for by the things that one loses. The rich possess much that the poor lack, while the poor often possess things that are beyond the reach of the rich."[83] This keeps everything in balance.

However, the Hermetists taught that this is not always the case with pleasure. Just because things are going great for you, this does not mean that you will ultimately have to pay for the pleasure with a negative experience. "The Law of Compensation is ever in operation, striving to balance and counter-balance, and always succeeding in time, even though several lives may be required for the return swing of the Pendulum of Rhythm."[84] This statement refers to reincarnation. The Hermetists state that if you experienced much pain in one life, then you could experience pleasure in another life.

It takes time to master the principle of rhythm, but as people learn to know themselves deeply and understand the rise and fall of emotions and feelings, they can better recognize their consciousness and learn to control their will. Moods and feelings come and go; life has its ups and downs. The

83. The Three Initiates, *The Kybalion*, 170.
84. The Three Initiates, *The Kybalion*, 170.

swing of the pendulum, according to the Hermetic principle of rhythm, will always compensate.

RHYTHM: THE FLOW OF LIFE

Throughout life, people experience the good with the bad. Each day has ups and downs as people experience the emotional pull of other people and of events. According to the Hermetic principle of rhythm, whatever happens during one day, one week, one month, one year, and so on, will fall back into balance as the pendulum swings.

Lisa Layden, who refers to herself as a thought leader, has sought to understand life since she was a girl. As she has educated herself about the inner workings of life, Layden has begun to share her information with the world in hopes of educating others to make a change. Once more people become aware of themselves and the world around them, they will better understand their purpose in life.

Before Layden's brother passed away, he spoke about life being like a roller coaster. Layden has taken his words to heart. She shares her understanding of his declaration: "It just means that, number one, it should be fun. Enjoy life," she insists, "even though there are ups and downs and twists and turns, because this is our opportunity to experience life as a human and all that goes with it."

Despite the turmoil life can throw at you and the hard times that come with it, embrace this time on earth. "It's just a small piece of essentially what and who we are. It's a very short experience in the span of human history. It's a very short experience in the span of the universe itself, so enjoy it as much as you can," Layden states.

What reality seems to show us is an incomplete picture. "We think in terms of good and bad, and right and wrong, and light and dark," Layden says. "At the end of the day, it's all the same." The Hermetic principle of polarity states that everything, both the good and the bad, is essentially the same but just a varying degree of the other. "We view our human experience through our five basic senses and through the filters of the beliefs and mindsets that we have in our mind. So just understanding all of that can help."

To see beyond misconceptions and misperceptions, one can begin an educational journey. This education can be based on facts and on unlearning previous perceptions once thought to be true. Most divisive issues in today's society, whether personal or professional, are symptoms of misunderstanding. "We are all the same human race," Layden states, adding that as the human race, people must start seeing themselves as one species and part of a collective on this planet. "I think we're all one," she shares. "It's like looking at a cell in your body and assuming that it's not a part of you. It is a part of you." This realization that everyone is connected is a belief that Hermes Trismegistus shared throughout his teachings.

Education will help those wanting to help themselves. Find books that resonate with you or register for classes that will help you grow from where you are. Finding your purpose will also help you become more in touch with life and your higher self. Layden calls it the "big why" or your purpose in life. "Stop thinking that it's your passion or your passions. It's not. And stop thinking that it's a career or a job or hobbies," she explains. These, Layden says, are simply vehicles to express your purpose. "At our very core, we all have the same big why," Layden states. "I think it's to understand that we are actually all collectively one. And that once we understand that, we can have so much more balance on this playground that I call earth."

Layden says the mind wants two things, to survive and to thrive, which can affect perceptions and thoughts. Society plays its part, cajoling people to reach for immediate gratification instead of focusing on individual self-awareness or the bigger picture of the collective whole. So how can you increase your own consciousness to regain balance within the Hermetic principle of rhythm? Layden suggests enjoying the time you have on earth. "Love yourself and love others," she says.

TAKEAWAYS

1. Everyone is part of one human race.

2. Enjoy the twists and turns of life because it is only a short span of time.

3. Be a better individual to create a better collective whole.

4. Education is the key to understanding.

5. Love yourself and love others.

WAYS TO BENEFIT FROM RHYTHM IN DAILY LIFE

The Hermetic masters learned to control the ebb and flow of situations to control the principle of rhythm within their own lives. If you feel down or depressed, help is available to learn to cope with these emotions and feel more uplifted. Becoming aware of thoughts and emotions, using techniques to gain control of yourself, and working in service to others can help you deal with the ups and downs of life. Bad times will happen. But remember that the negative experience is simply the backward swing of the pendulum, and better times are ahead. Go with the flow.

The principle of rhythm manifests in the physical and spiritual states, as well as the mental state. Master the principle of rhythm to gain better control of your feelings, moods, and emotions, and to grasp reality more easily when you are experiencing uncontrollable or unstable situations. Learning to control your thoughts and actions can create more stability for everyone involved.

There are many ways to incorporate the Hermetic principle of rhythm into daily life. Learning to control emotion through breathwork, enjoying the rhythm of music, and discovering a sense of gratitude during service to others are just a few avenues to pursue to reach self-awareness and master the principle of rhythm.

BALANCE THE HEART, BALANCE THE MIND

One way to balance physical, mental, and spiritual well being is to incorporate the scientifically proven HeartMath® system into daily life. Rollin McCraty, PhD, serves as the director of research at HeartMath®, Inc. and states that the revolutionary system can help a person self-regulate and become more self-aware of emotions. "Emotions really run the show. They are the primary drivers of the activity in our nervous system, in our hormonal system," McCraty shares. "Our basic research back in the early '90s was the first to show that what we feel, our emotions, are best reflected in the rhythms of the heart, literally."

Heart rate variability (HRV), or the varying time between heartbeats, is lowered by stress or naturally with age. A lower HRV can lead to disease. "When we're feeling things like frustration, or anxiety, or overwhelmed, impatience," McCraty shares, "the rhythm becomes what we call inco-herent." When someone focuses on feelings of appreciation, gratitude, care, and so on, the body systems synchronize, and the HRV resumes a coherent state. The HeartMath® system teaches people to attain a coherent heart rhythm at will.

In the study of psychophysiology, doctors have found the heart sends neuro signals to the brain, affecting brain functions. "When we're in a coherent [heart] rhythm, the brain is interpreting that as everything is safe," McCraty explains. "It literally synchronizes the neural activity in the brain, so when we're in a coherent state, you have faster reaction times, better coordination, better capacity to self-regulate, to think clearly, make good decisions." With practice, a person can refocus energy and reach a "heart coherent" state even while experiencing impatience or frustration.

Many of the HeartMath® programs are based on energy models. "What drains unnecessary energy for most people on the planet is emotions, unmanaged emotions," McCraty explains. The HeartMath Experience includes a series of videos outlining techniques such as the Quick Coherence® Technique.

THE QUICK COHERENCE® TECHNIQUE

Step 1. Focus your attention in the area of the heart. Imagine your breath is flowing in and out of your heart or chest area, breathing a little slower and deeper than usual. Find an easy rhythm that is comfortable.

Step 2. As you continue heart-focused breathing, make a sincere attempt to experience a regenerative feeling, such as appreciation or care for someone or something in your life. *HeartMath is a registered trademark of Quantum Intech, Inc. For all HeartMath trademarks go to www.heartmath.com/trademarks.*

If practiced correctly, this simple process can help a person manage negative emotions, feel better physically and mentally, and experience more clarity.

THE RHYTHM OF MUSIC

Music can feed the spirit, calm the mind, be exhilarating during exercise, spark a distant memory, or entice someone to the dance floor. Is it the beat or the rhythm that moves you? Is it the vibration of the melodies emitting from the speaker system that can stabilize or boost mood? Is it the nostalgia you feel or the memories that are triggered when you hear a certain song? Whatever it may be, music is a beneficial part of life.

Music can improve every aspect of living. "Physical, mental, emotional—all of our developmental dimensions—are affected by music or can be affected by music," explains

Dena Register, PhD, MT-BC, and regulatory affairs advisor for the Certification Board for Music Therapists. As a board-certified music therapist, Register uses music with every age group, and the benefits are ultimately driven by the individual. These benefits include promoting rehabilitation, enhancing memory, or allowing a person to express emotion.

"A lot of the focus right now is based on brain response and neurologic behavior and how we use the music to then alter what is happening," Register points out. For example, someone who has suffered a stroke could use music therapy during rehabilitation. "The way the music behaves in the brain or the brain behaves as a result of the music, and where the different aspects of music [are] stored," Register explains, "allows someone to achieve greater results, often. It's such an example, I think, of how embedded music is."

The response to music is different for each individual. "Sometimes there isn't a memory associated, and it's just the way we respond to music." For example, a baby who is at the stage of cruising—not quite walking but can pull up on the edge of a couch—may begin to "dance" if an upbeat song begins to play. "They will move to the beat of the music. They bounce up and down because the brain says, 'Oh, there's the beat. I found the beat. I'm going to move to that,'" Register states. She believes instincts and brain response drive an individual to move to the rhythm. As a person ages and experiences life, more layers are created in relation to music, so memories, experiences, mood, emotions, and so on, are brought into the musical equation. Studies are ongoing to determine how music is processed in the brain, where it is stored, and why it has certain effects on each individual.

Patients with Alzheimer's disease or dementia can be helped by music therapy as well. Many times, a patient can recall every word of a song or play a song from childhood on the piano. "It's a way to tap back into experiences that we've had, and like everything in life, you've got the shadow side and the light side." The light side of the memory is positive. "The shadow side being if we have a musical component that is associated with something that is traumatic, that can also be triggering and can immediately get us back in that space," Register explains.

There are so many layers of how music can affect a listener. It is critical for a music therapist to know how to change the music in response to the physical and emotional reactions of the patient. A board-certified music therapist typically performs live music, but recorded songs are also used in therapy. If the performance is live, the music therapist can alter the music, thus changing the experience for the person receiving therapy.

Patient-preferred music, which is determined based on information received from the family or the patient, is used during treatment. If a patient is in pain or having a hard time getting settled in bed, Register typically starts with a more assertive, louder, up-tempo song from the patient-preferred list, and then gradually changes the musical elements to calm the mood. "What you'll find is that people's bodies and brains respond to that. So I could take a patient who was uncomfortable and moving around in their bed from that state to fully asleep by the time I left them 30 or 45 minutes later. So altering those components are what we look for if we're working with a patient." A music therapist meets the patients at their current state and then uses music to improve their state, physically and mentally.

A person seeking music therapy can search for a professional, but anyone can take advantage of the benefits of music. "I think it's that self-meditative piece of really listening deeply to something and what it is that you like about a particular piece of music," Register explains. Think about what kinds of elements in music change your mental state to a preferred mood, and find more artists or similar songs that feature these elements. With the availability of any type of music at your fingertips through technology, more people are using music and creating go-to playlists for various moods.

Those seeking musical benefits should pay attention to their sound environment, which is often overlooked. "The sound environment really makes a big difference," Register says. Pay attention to competing background noise. For example, the television at home is on full volume, the children are arguing, the dog is barking, and another family member is playing a video on the phone. These sounds compete with each other and can create an uncomfortable and agitating environment. "Thinking about that when you're selecting music for yourself, I think, makes a really big difference. We come into the world inherently musical," Register asserts. For some, especially in their younger years, music is fostered, but along the way, that passion for music may get lost. "Someone says, 'Please sing softer,' or 'Please don't sing,' or 'Well, you're not really very good at that,'" Register points out. But Register wants people to understand that engaging in music, especially live music, is helpful on many levels. Whether it is attending a concert, singing camp songs, playing the piano, or drumming to the beat of a favorite song, that engagement has positive effects. "I think if I had a message for the world, it would be, engage in live music, sing, and play. Those aspects are incredibly beneficial for us as humans, for us individually, but as a collective as well."

SERVICE TO OTHERS

Serving others and giving to others can provide a sense of gratitude, happiness, and connection. According to the Hermetic principle of rhythm, giving means receiving. Whether it is providing a service for which you receive a tangible return, or it is volunteering time for the sheer gratification of helping another, you gain when you give. Seeing the joy on a child's face while opening a birthday gift, realizing that a kind word or a smile brightened someone's day, or providing a meal, clothing, or school supplies to someone who needs them: these make life more joyous for the receiver, and the giver also experiences joy.

In the Bible, Luke 6:38 states, "Give, and it shall be given unto you."[85] The giver may not actually receive anything tangible on the physical plane but will receive something on the mental or spiritual plane. If you feel thankful and blessed for being the cause of another's happiness, then you

---

85. *The Holy Bible, King James Version*, 853.

may be more inclined to continue helping and serving others throughout life.

Acts 20:35 in the Bible says, "I have shewed you all things, how that so labouring ye ought to support the weak, and to remember the words of the Lord Jesus, how he said, It is more blessed to give than to receive."[86] In other words, there is joy in the act of giving when it is done with a pure motive. Giving can be beneficial for both the giver and the recipient. The giver could receive joy simply by causing another's joy. The person on the receiving end of a good deed or support could feel thankful, which in turn, could impel that person to do something nice for someone else, paying it forward. For example, if a driver in line at a drive-through restaurant pays for the order of the customer in the car behind them, then that person might choose to pay for the customer behind them, and so on. One act of kindness could lead to hundreds of acts of kindness in one day.

There are many ways to serve and support others. You can share knowledge and experience with a loved one, friend, or colleague to guide them through a difficult time, or you can lend a helping hand to a friend who is moving their household. When deciding how you can serve others and give back

---

86. *The Holy Bible, King James Version*, 928.

to the community, find something you enjoy doing. Parents can get their children involved in volunteering. This habit of giving will continue to be cultivated throughout life if it is instilled at a young age. Whether it is cooking and serving Thanksgiving dinner at a local shelter, delivering toiletries to the local homeless population, writing cards to members of the military serving abroad, spending time playing card games at a local assisted living facility, sorting clothing at a donation center, volunteering to teach Sunday school or Vacation Bible School at church, or walking dogs or playing with cats waiting to be adopted at an animal shelter, you have unlimited possibilities to serve others. And serving others ultimately benefits the giver with feelings of hope, accomplishment, love, and gratitude.

The feeling or attitude of gratitude, or thankfulness, can help calm the mind and the spirit. A study, "Counting Blessings Versus Burdens: An Experimental Investigation of Gratitude and Subjective Well-Being in Daily Life,"[87] suggests that if a person consciously focuses on blessings, this could have emotional benefits. Researchers studied how a "grateful outlook"

87. Robert A. Emmons and Michael E. McCullough, "Counting Blessings Versus Burdens: An Experimental Investigation of Gratitude and Subjective Well-Being in Daily Life," *Journal of Personality and Social Psychology* 84, no. 2 (2003): 377–89, https://doi.org/10.1037/0022-3514.84.2.377.

and the act of "counting one's blessings" can lead to greater happiness and physical well-being. Participants were asked to keep records of gratitude-inducing experiences, hassles, and life events. Participants also rated their moods, coping behaviors, and physical symptoms related to each circumstance. Researchers then observed the psychological and physical well-being of participants based on their responses.

In the first group of participants, the study discovered that those who experienced gratitude were more optimistic and "reported fewer physical complaints and reported spending significantly more time exercising."[88] The second group of participants was given "a more intensive procedure for cultivating gratitude" that included comparing themselves to others. For example, participants were asked to keep track of how they were "better off than others" and how others have things that they did not have. Results showed that those who experienced greater levels of gratitude in their experiences had "helped someone with a personal problem or offered emotional support to another, suggesting prosocial motivation as a consequence of the gratitude induction."[89]

---

88. Emmons and McCullough, "Counting Blessings," 381.
89. Emmons and McCullough, "Counting Blessings," 383.

TAKEAWAYS

1. Look for ways to be grateful every day.

2. Serve others.

3. Give more.

4. If you give, then you shall receive.

5. Being grateful leads to greater physical and psychological well-being.

Chapter 12

PRINCIPLE 6: THE PRINCIPLE OF CAUSATION

*Rather than studying the laws of cause
and effect, people spend their lives being
the effect and running from the cause.*

—Eugene J. Martin, visual artist

Everything happens for a reason. Every incident in life is either a cause or an effect. *The Kybalion* states that the principle of causation governs all. Each occurrence is either a cause or an effect of a cause or a series of causes. According to *The Kybalion*, nothing is a coincidence or chance. What some consider chance is actually "an expression of an obscure cause," which is a cause that is neither perceived nor understood—and might never be determined.

Regarding cause and effect, how dice fall when they are thrown may appear to be chance, but many aspects play a role in which numbers appear on the black and white cubes. The law of averages, which is basically finding balance with past and future events, can play a role, but causes that can affect the final landing position of the dice could be the energy expended with the throw, the texture of the table, and how the dice hit the table.

Understanding the Hermetic principle of causation allows people to become more self-aware and take action to heal their lives. Everything a person experiences throughout life shapes who they become. Many choose to learn and grow from their experiences, while others may find themselves stuck in ill-favored patterns. If you can truly discover what caused certain feelings or actions, then you can have more control over effects and future events.

> *Every Cause has its Effect; every Effect has its Cause; everything happens according to Law; Chance is but a name for Law not recognized; there are many planes of causation, but nothing escapes the Law.*
> —The Kybalion

One example of the principle of causation in *The Kybalion* is the collapse of a roof. The Three Initiates point out that rain can cause a rock to slide down a hill, the rock can crash into a roof, and the roof, especially if it was already unsteady, might collapse. The series of causes ultimately leads to the effect: the roof collapses.

The Hermetic principle of causation continues the order of the universe. Every event is linked to the event that follows it, and everything—past, present, and future—is related. Every thought and every action fit into the principle of causation. The thought or action is either a cause or an effect. *The Kybalion* states that "[t]he underlying Principle of Cause and Effect has been accepted as correct by practically all the thinkers of the world worthy of the name."[90]

HOW YOU CAN BENEFIT FROM CAUSE AND EFFECT

Nothing happens by coincidence. What happens is supposed to happen. Some call it fate. Hermes Trismegistus writes of fate in *The Corpus Hermeticum*. Although *The Kybalion* does not mention fate, it does say that to disbelieve the principle

90. The Three Initiates, *The Kybalion*, 172.

of cause and effect "would be to take the phenomena of the universe from the domain of Law and Order, and to relegate it to the control of the imaginary something which men have called 'Chance.'"[91]

Many believe in karma, a principle in Buddhism and Hinduism in which a person's actions affect fate, or what happens to them in the future. Although karma is not mentioned in *The Kybalion*, it is essentially the same thing as the cycle of cause and effect. The Hermetic principle of causation refers to how an action affects another, and so on.

If your great-great-grandparents had not met one hundred years ago, the next generations, including you, would not have existed. This is truth. Based on an assertion in *The Kybalion*, the act of the author in writing this section of *The Little Book of Hermetic Principles* and the act of the reader in reading this section of the book will affect both the author and the reader, "but will also have a direct, or indirect, effect upon many other people now living and who will live in the ages to come."[92] How? The specifics are impossible to predict. But maybe the Hermetic principle of causation will give you, the reader, more focus on how to become a cause of

---

91. The Three Initiates, *The Kybalion*, 172.
92. The Three Initiates, *The Kybalion*, 179.

success. You might choose a different path in life, one that ultimately leads to abundance, thus benefiting yourself and future generations.

Every thought or action of yours fits into cause and effect. Everyone who makes an appearance in your life is there for a reason. Opening yourself to the understanding that cause brings about effect—and that this is law—allows you to see how an action creates an effect, beneficial or not, on yourself or others. You can thus take the necessary steps to create effects that are beneficial.

BE THE CAUSE INSTEAD OF BECOMING THE EFFECT

With every experience in life, you can deal with cause and effect by learning effective techniques and tools. If you truly work to determine how one event may have led to another—the cause and the effect—then you can continue to improve yourself, your relationships, your opportunities, and so on.

Various self-improvement techniques can aid you as you travel the road to understanding the principle of cause and effect. Yoga, meditation, inspirational and self-help books, and continuing education will help those searching for an understanding of how to improve and be more present in daily life.

"Given the same causes, the same results will follow."[93] In other words, if you want to change yourself, you must make the effort to change. Trying something new could lead to a new career, a new relationship, a new hobby, or a new experience, which could itself lead to greater happiness, awareness, joy, love, and so on. If you want to change but never take the initiative to do anything differently, change will not happen, and you will keep getting the same results.

The Three Initiates do not delve deeply into either free will, which is the belief that you can choose your own path, or into the other end of the spectrum, that your life is controlled by fate. *The Kybalion*, regarding the principle of polarity, states that both beliefs are half-truths. Instead, "man may be both Free and yet bound by Necessity."[94] The ancient Hermetists held this to be true: "The further the creation is from the Centre, the more it is bound; the nearer the Centre it reaches, the nearer Free is it."[95] The more you are aware of the control you hold within yourself, the freer you will be.

---

93. The Three Initiates, *The Kybalion*, 175.
94. The Three Initiates, *The Kybalion*, 179.
95. The Three Initiates, *The Kybalion*, 179.

You can learn to manifest freedom by realizing what affects you and how you can change these causes into more positive outcomes. The causes might be heredity, your living or work environment, your thoughts, your desires, your emotions, and so on. Or the causes could be the billboard displaying a new car, which leads you to spend unnecessarily, or the smell of freshly baked cookies wafting onto the sidewalk, which leads you to eat more sugar than is good for you. Many people believe they have made decisions or choices freely. But environmental influences led them to make those decisions or choices because they sparked a desire within. "Moved like the pawns on the checkerboard of life, they play their parts."[96]

Instead of allowing the environment or suggestions from others to influence you to take action or feel a certain way, exercise your own will. *The Kybalion* states that humans can rise above the materialistic plane to a higher plane by becoming aware of the higher power within and the truth that one can learn to control thoughts and moods, "and thus became the Movers in the game, instead of Pawns—Causes instead of Effects."[97]

---

96. The Three Initiates, *The Kybalion*, 181.
97. The Three Initiates, *The Kybalion*, 181.

TO SELF-IMPROVE, LOOK INSIDE FOR ANSWERS

The first step toward self-improvement is acknowledging that change is essential. If you want to improve any aspect of your life, you must first determine the problem or the pattern you want to change, make a plan, and then act.

Maybe you are afraid of commitment or failure. Maybe the fear is that once a goal is accomplished, the future is uncertain, so you never even attempt to reach the goal. To realize what is causing these fears or emotions, think about why you are afraid or why you feel a certain way. What led to certain destructive behaviors? What "cause" led to this effect? Was it a specific trauma? It may not be easy, especially with deep-rooted issues, and it may take time, but in the end, it is worth the search to determine what is causing unnecessary internal strife and make changes. Once you determine what is causing fear, sadness, anxiety, and so on, it is easier to come to terms with the issue, learn from it, and ultimately take action to make necessary changes.

The principle of causation can also be implemented by determining what you want out of life and creating a plan to accomplish the envisioned goal. A goal is the effect of a cause or chain of causes. If your goal is to earn more money, then determine what must be done to cause a higher income. The answer could be returning to school for a degree or certification in a field that pays more. The chain of causes would continue by applying for employment, interviewing, and then accepting a more lucrative job offer.

Becoming more self-aware oftentimes includes questioning yourself about aspects of your life. Why do you feel or think a certain way? What do you want out of life? How can you accomplish these dreams and goals? Focus on becoming the cause of the effect you want to embody. It could lead to astonishing outcomes.

BE PRESENT IN EVERY SITUATION

To become more aware of cause and effect, be fully present in every situation. Sometimes it can be difficult to be present. There is always a stray thought, a random noise, or social media, which can suck attention away from what is important.

Technology is a huge culprit when it comes to absence of mind in any situation: the children playing on their phones at dinnertime, the mother distracted by the computer as her child shares a story, or the friend checking a quick text during a conversation. Many situations involving the continual presence of technology lead to the absence of physical, mental, or emotional presence.

A 2003 report, "The Benefits of Being Present: Mindfulness and Its Role in Psychological Well-Being,"[98] reviews the importance of mindfulness, or the conscious action of being aware and attentive in present reality. "Mindfulness captures a quality of consciousness that is characterized by clarity and vividness of current experience and functioning and thus stands in contrast to the mindless, less 'awake' states of habitual or automatic functioning that may be chronic for many individuals."[99]

Several studies in the report determined the Mindful Attention Awareness Scale (MAAS) scores of participants based in part on answers to specific questions. Participants rated how often they were forgetful, careless, or did things automatically according to a scale (almost always = 1 to almost

98. Kirk Brown and Richard Ryan, "The Benefits of Being Present: Mindfulness and Its Role in Psychological Well-Being," *Journal of Personality and Social Psychology* 84, no. 4 (2003): 822–48, https://doi.org/10.1037/0022-3514.84.4.822
99. Brown and Ryan, "Being Present," 823.

never = 6). Higher MAAS scores showed the participants to be "more aware of and receptive to inner experiences" and "more 'in tune' with their emotional states,"[100] allowing the participants to have more ability to alter their emotional states. The MAAS score was "strongly related to clarity of emotional states but also with mood repair."[101] The report points out that those with a higher MAAS score were less self-conscious and socially anxious compared with those who scored lower on the scale. Ultimately, the research supports the role that mindfulness plays in fostering psychological well-being and aiding a person in self-regulation.

Being present is advantageous, especially in regard to relationships and communication. A child who knows a parent is actually giving full attention to a story about finding the perfect rock in the creek, the home run hit during the neighborhood baseball game, or the project presentation at school is more likely to engage the parent in other conversations. These conversations could be about life plans, hopes, or dreams, but they could also include other serious conversations about peer pressure, sex, or bullying.

---

100. Brown and Ryan, "Being Present," 832.
101. Brown and Ryan, "Being Present," 828.

Being present when a partner is sharing feelings or a concern can lead to understanding on both sides. Being present when a boss is explaining a new product or service can lead not only to knowledge but to mutual respect. Being present, instead of acting on impulse or out of habit, in any situation gives you a well-rounded overview of what is actually happening and can allow you the opportunity to ask pertinent questions. If you are present, you gain a better understanding of the cause of a disagreement or the effect of inattention. This allows you to more fully grasp all aspects of the experience.

Chapter 13

PRINCIPLE 7: THE PRINCIPLE OF GENDER

The union of feminine and masculine energies within the individual is the basis of all creation.
—Shakti Gawain, author

According to the Hermetic principle of gender in *The Kybalion*, everything has both masculine and feminine qualities. These qualities are not biological characteristics, such as sex organs or the physical body of a man or woman, but more the character traits of the person, the energetic qualities that the person exudes. *The Kybalion* states that the masculine quality is considered positive and the act of being, while the feminine is considered negative and the act of becoming. This is not to say that the female gender or a person who displays more feminine qualities is negative in personality or mood. It has more to do with how the energies work.

For example, an atom is created when electrons (negative energy) are drawn to the positive nucleus, created from protons (positive energy) and neutrons (neutral energy). The electrons begin vibrating rapidly around the positive pole, or the nucleus, creating an atom. The resulting atom was created from both masculine and feminine energy, so it will always contain both genders as part of the whole.

> *Gender is in everything; everything has*
> *its Masculine and Feminine Principles;*
> *Gender manifests on all planes.*
> —The Kybalion

According to *The Kybalion*, gender is solely about creating. Once matter is formed, it contains both genders, masculine and feminine energies, and always will include both genders, or positive and negative energies. The masculine, or positive, energy does not mean strong, and the feminine, or negative, energy does not mean weak. The negative (feminine) electron seeks to unite with the positive (masculine) pole of an atom. The feminine energy is known as the creative energy, and it vibrates around the masculine pole to create the atom.

The science of atomic creation offers proof of existence of the Hermetic principle of gender. *The Kybalion* states that this well-known phenomena exists regarding "the 'attraction and repulsion' of the atoms; chemical affinity; the 'loves and hates' of the atomic particles; the attraction or cohesion between the molecules of matter. These facts are too well known to need extended comment from us. But, have you ever considered that all of these things are manifestations of the Gender Principle?"[102]

EMBRACING DIFFERENCES

As the Hermetic principle of gender states, each person has both masculine and feminine qualities, or energies. These qualities are not about the genitalia of the person but rather the characteristics and energies displayed. The principle of gender can be understood in conjunction with the principle of polarity, which states that everything is a degree of its opposite. Every person exhibits both masculine and feminine qualities to varying degrees.

These gender qualities are also reflected in the Hermetic principles of mentalism and rhythm. One day, a person

---

102. The Three Initiates, *The Kybalion*, 191.

may feel very creative; the next day, the same person may have writer's block. A person could be more focused and deadline-driven one day and prefer to sit around the house relaxing the next. An individual could be more emotional on any given day and then not so emotional later that week.

People can begin to see these gender qualities in others once they are aware of their own masculine and feminine qualities, or energies, and are on the path of personal growth. Before you judge another based on masculine or feminine qualities, you must figuratively "walk a mile in another's shoes" to truly understand that person.

INCORPORATING MASCULINITY AND FEMININITY INTO EVERYDAY LIFE

Self-awareness drives growth. The ability to self-reflect and understand your triggers, the possible effects of your actions, and how to control your emotions offers you the chance to rise above disagreeable or displeasing situations, which could have a negative impact. Understanding that every person on this planet has both masculine and feminine qualities within can help in situations in which communication and acknowledgment are necessary.

People, regardless of sex or how they act or react, can reflect both gender qualities. A woman might be assertive, which is thought to be a more "masculine" attribute, in certain situations to share her thoughts or desires. This quality might come across to some as demanding and might be seen in a negative light. But this woman is simply expressing herself, which is her right as a human being, in hopes of acknowledgment. A man might become emotional after a meaningful or tragic experience. He might cry. Does this make him any less of a man? No. He is expressing emotion, which might be thought a more "feminine" quality, allowing him the opportunity to express feelings, find comfort in a difficult situation, and grow through the experience.

Whatever the situation, unless safety is an issue—whether physical, mental, or emotional—people deserve to be heard and recognized. This does not mean that you must tolerate the behavior of someone who is aggressive or exhibiting emotional or mental unrest. The issue can be addressed at a later time when all parties are calmer. The principle of gender simply states that each person has what are considered to be both masculine and feminine qualities. And if you are on a journey of personal growth, then you must recognize these masculine or feminine qualities apparent within yourself and make an effort to gain access to qualities of the other gender to remain in balance. Acknowledging others and their thoughts, needs, desires, and so on, will also help you continue on your journey of personal development.

BECOMING MORE ASSERTIVE

Assertiveness could be considered a masculine quality, and it might not come easy for some. But this trait can be cultivated. Many times, people don't understand that there is a difference between assertiveness and aggressiveness. Assertive behavior is self-assured and confident, while aggressive behavior is an attack or a confrontation. An aggressive action is often unkind, harsh, or ill-intentioned. Aggressive people may use tone, words, or body language to put down the other person just to make themselves feel better, while people who are assertive advocate for themselves in a non-aggressive manner.

Joree Rose, MA, LMFT, author, owner of the Mindfulness and Therapy Center, and host of the podcast *Journey Forward with Joree Rose*, believes many people, especially women, shy away from being assertive for fear of being called bossy or rude. "To me, assertiveness is embodying the either mental, emotional, or physical posture of holding that sacred ground, speaking your truth, standing in your honor, and in your sense of self," Rose explains.

"When I don't speak up, when I don't hold that sacred ground, I feel unseen, I feel unheard, I don't feel validated, I don't feel acknowledged," Rose states. "I feel like my soul is slowly dying inside because I am withering away for fear that if I do speak my truth, if I do hold that ground, I'm going to be rejected, denied, or ignored."

Self-awareness allows for positive change. It is often difficult to learn a new skill, especially when the opposite has been part of you for a lifetime. If you believe that change is difficult or impossible, then you will remain in that cycle. This refers back to the Hermetic principle of mentalism. But change is possible, and the recognition and compassion that the journey of change could be a difficult experience allows for self-acceptance. The opposite of compassion is judgment. "If we stay in that judgment where our inner critic is taking over, it's easy to stay stuck there because we're going to feed upon that judgment," Rose explains. "To have compassion for ourselves is to say, 'Yeah, this is really, really hard.' And I can still practice this, and maybe I can take these baby steps toward creating this change."

A possible reason for holding back on speaking your truth is the fear that you will not be acknowledged or validated. But not advocating for yourself can create a disconnect within relationships and create an inner critic. If others do not validate your truth, then you will begin to invalidate that truth. But one day it could become apparent that holding back no longer serves you. "At some point, the benefit outweighs the cost….[S]peaking up will allow me to have a better chance at being seen, heard, and validated than just staying quiet and not saying my truth at all," Rose says. "I think everybody, child or adult, no matter how old we are, we all want to be seen, heard, and validated. In [the] absence of being seen, heard, and validated, we do one of two things. We get louder or we shut down, both of which keep us disconnected." But everyone has the capability to change these patterns into something better.

To change a meeker, more passive quality into a more assertive one, you must first understand how the brain and body work. The body's natural defense system protects you against a potential threat with a response of fight, flight, or freeze. "Our sympathetic nervous system gets activated, and we feel physiologically the effects of that. We feel the heart race. We feel the [sinking in the] pit [of] the stomach. We feel the tightness in the throat, the heaviness on our chest, the tension in our shoulders. And that's an indication that my nervous system is activated right now." The response of fight, flight, or freeze could be a reaction to a real threat, but this response could also be activated by simply the thought that someone wants to harm you. "When you start to notice that physiology get activated, that's a really great opportunity to practice some self-care, that inner self-talk," Rose shares. Once you become self-aware during the interaction, taking one breath at a time can help you return your physiology to a calmer state. Acknowledge and accept the emotion, fear, and so on, but then let go of the emotions that may not be beneficial. It is not always easy to accept something that is uncomfortable or difficult, but it is necessary in order to move forward.

Rose thinks of being assertive and standing in your truth in terms of a martial arts stance, a physical posture in which a person could be knocked down only with difficulty. For example, a person's feet may be spread apart slightly, knees bent, with one foot in front of the other. This stance allows the person to stand strong in truth and to balance energy. "I literally think about embodying that stance versus if you were just to stand upright with your arms down by your sides, someone could easily just knock you down and that would be not enacting your power."

To become more assertive, try a new pattern but keep the opportunity to pull back to safety if necessary. Humans are sensitive beings and should give themselves and others a little grace. This grace allows for a deeper understanding of another's truths and adds to your ability to learn and grow in the process.

Rose did not always have an assertive personality, and this hindered her from sharing her needs with others. Her divorce empowered her to honor her truth, and she found her voice. Rose says she realized that she was worthy of expressing her needs, and that becoming more assertive has helped her personally and professionally. "My worthiness is not dependent upon my partner meeting my needs. I am only in control of myself. So I also had to learn that the practice was in the speaking up, honoring myself, speaking my truth," Rose points out. "The success of that did not come from what happened once I said it. I could not control how someone else was going to receive it and what they were going to do with it, but I taught myself the power is in the action that I can take."

Being more assertive with strangers is a good way to practice speaking up for yourself, but always keep safety in mind. "If a stranger is crossing our boundary, if a stranger is violating a value of ours, then what a great opportunity to practice," Rose says. She also suggests that people working on the skill of assertiveness inform close family and friends about their journey, possibly sharing that they will be shifting how they show up in conversation or interactions. In time, with a little practice and self-awareness, being assertive gets easier.

TAKEAWAYS

1. Be aware of your needs and desires.

2. Be aware of the thoughts and feelings that arise during your interactions with others.

3. Do not be afraid to speak your truth.

4. Practice the skill of assertiveness.

5. Be assertive without being aggressive.

IT IS POSSIBLE TO FEEL EMPATHY

Oftentimes people confuse sympathy and empathy. Sympathy is feeling sorrow for another's misfortune, while empathy is the ability to understand what the other person is going through and share these feelings. Being empathetic could be seen as a more feminine energy, but people of all genders can exhibit this trait. If you do not have a strong sense of empathy, you can learn to be more empathetic, allowing you to better understand others.

Humans are social by nature, and the presence and support of others can help lead people to their highest and greatest good. The ability to understand another's feelings and perceptions can build stronger relationships. Roman Krznaric, author of *Empathy: Why It Matters, and How to Get It* and founder of the Empathy Museum, believes humans are capable of cultivating empathy. Krznaric authored an article, "Six Habits of Highly Empathetic People," in which he outlines avenues people can try in order to build their empathy. "We can nurture its growth throughout our lives—and we can use it as a radical force for social transformation,"[103] Krznaric states in the article.

One way you can be more empathetic is to be inquisitive about others. Ask questions, actually listen to the answers, and you will learn more about family, friends, and strangers that cross your path. To be more empathetic, you can also challenge beliefs or prejudices you may have about others

103. Roman Krznaric, "Six Habits of Highly Empathetic People," *Greater Good Magazine*, November 27, 2012, https:// greatergood. berkeley.edu/article/item/six_habits_of_highly _empathic_people1.

based on religion, race, politics, social status, and so on, and try to find common ground. The human race is one race.

You may not understand what another person is going through if you have not had a similar experience. And even then, these experiences might differ because you and the other person might have different backgrounds, knowledge, abilities to control emotions, prejudices, and so on. So how can you be more empathetic?

Empathy may seem impossible for some, but the ability to open up and be more aware of the feelings and energies of others will allow you to see others for who they truly are, not just what you perceive them to be. To have more empathy, take a little time to understand how the person is feeling or what the person is going through during a time of need. Think back to a time when you had a similar situation or a similar feeling.

When showing empathy, advice is not always necessary. Empathy is showing support during a time of another's discomfort. A hug, a gentle squeeze of the hand, or a pat on the back could ease the pain. A kind word, a smile, or a simple, "I understand," could provide the person in distress a boost of hope.

Brené Brown, PhD, LMSW, research professor at the University of Houston and author of *Daring Greatly*, says, "Empathy is a strange and powerful thing. There is no script. There is no right way or wrong way to do it. It's simply listening, holding space, withholding judgment, emotionally connecting, and communicating that incredibly healing message of 'you're not alone.'"[104] Empathy can be challenging, but it is possible to be more in tune with others. It may seem overwhelming at times, especially as the world population of more than seven billion continues to grow, but positive change must happen in order to build a sustainable life for all on this planet. Change begins with being aware of yourself, as well as others.

CREATIVITY

The act of creating, according to *The Kybalion*, is feminine (negative) energy vibrating around masculine (positive) energy. The creation of the atom is a perfect example of how the principle of gender works. It takes both genders to create.

---

104. Brené Brown, *Daring Greatly: How the Courage to Be Vulnerable Transforms the Way We Live, Love, Parent, and Lead* (New York: Gotham Books, 2012), 81.

In today's world, there is an endless supply of information available to learn a new skill and start a journey toward being more creative. Creativity is not just a word to describe artistic creations. Creativity comes in all forms: building a structure, developing a new product or recipe, growing a plant, and so on.

The Kybalion states, "THE UNIVERSE, AND ALL IT CONTAINS, IS A MENTAL CREATION OF THE ALL. Verily, indeed, ALL IS MIND!"[105] *The Kybalion* also asserts that when someone creates something, that person is actually part of the creation. "In other words, the entire virtue, life, spirit, of reality in the mental image is derived from the 'immanent mind' of the thinker."[106] The creation comes from the mind of the creator, so the creation is and always was part of the creator. This notion refers to the principle of correspondence: what is created on the mental plane becomes perceived reality on the physical plane.

So paint, draw, build, plant, sculpt, play, grow, and learn. Create a better version of yourself, which will ultimately help create a better world for the human race.

---

105. The Three Initiates, *The Kybalion*, 70.
106. The Three Initiates, *The Kybalion*, 97.

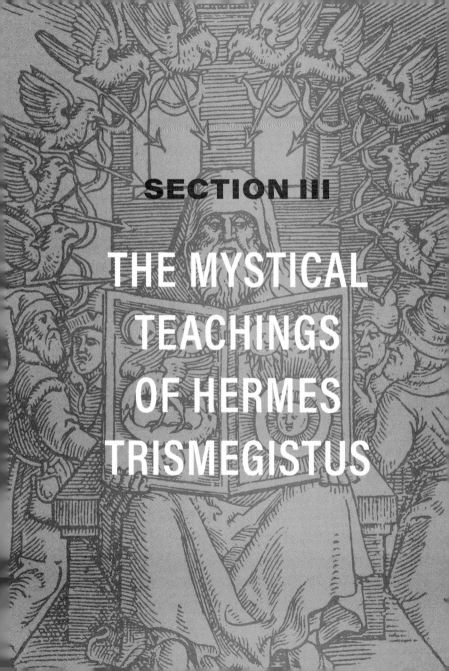

SECTION III

THE MYSTICAL TEACHINGS OF HERMES TRISMEGISTUS

This section includes Hermes Trismegistus' mystical teachings on astrology, alchemy, and magic. For some, these aspects of Trismegistus' teachings could be construed as unbelievable or even blasphemous. But throughout Trismegistus' credited teachings, he discusses the importance of living a pious, or spiritual and righteous, life. This, he says, is the only way to become one with God, the Father, the Creator of all. These supernatural fields are often verified by scientific evidence and natural law. In the following chapters, you will learn more about the ancient, traditional teachings of astrology, alchemy, and magic, and how they have evolved over the millennia.

Chapter 14

ASTROLOGY

For thousands of years, cultures have looked to the skies for guidance regarding crops, hunting, birth, and even war. They have used complicated methods to chart the alignment of the planets, star patterns, sun, and moon to help them make these decisions. For example, the Mayans timed their warfare based on the heliacal rising of the planet Venus, so when Venus rose before the sun, the Mayans could see the planet and believed it was a good time to start warfare. In ancient times, astrology was seen as a science, but now many people believe astrology is mystical. Traditional astrology included information about when events should or would happen, based on celestial alignment, and often outlined negative possibilities. Astrology has evolved over the millennia. Most modern astrology is psychological or based on characteristics related to a natal chart, as well as includes more positive or upbeat predictions.

The most common astrology in the modern world is that of the twelve zodiac signs, or sun signs. These astrological signs are based on the astral element alignment on a person's date of birth and are diagrammed in a natal chart. More aspects are often interpreted during a modern astrological reading, including moon signs, time of birth, and so on. But modern astrology is often considered less complicated than the astrology of ancient times. Hermes Trismegistus refers to the cosmos, sun, moon, planets, and stars in his writings, including *The Corpus Hermeticum*.

ASTROLOGICAL TEACHINGS OF HERMES TRISMEGISTUS AND TRADITIONAL ASTROLOGY

Hermes Trismegistus was a teacher of astrology, and although many astrological principles he is credited with having recorded have been around for thousands of years, he is often referred to as the founder of astrology. *The Centiloquium of Hermes Trismegistus* includes one hundred astrological treatises, or generalities. *A Centiloquium of Ptolemy* also exists, containing similar astrological information. The one hundred astrological truths credited to Trismegistus include information about the most favorable times to wed, travel, loan money, and begin a business or relationship. They also outline how to treat others and act depending on the alignment of celestial bodies.

Christopher Warnock, author, professional astrologer, and attorney, has studied and practiced traditional astrology, or medieval and Renaissance astrology, for more than two decades. "One of my key roles has been to help revive traditional astrological magic," he says. Warnock's interest in astrology began during his research of different spiritual paths. There are many different types of astrology, including modern, medieval, Renaissance, Hellenistic, Vedic, and Chinese. Traditional astrology includes more techniques and is more complex than modern astrology. "It's like having a whole golf bag full of golf clubs for every circumstance, as opposed to just walking around with a putter," Warnock explains. "So modern astrology is a kind of very, very simplified [approach]."

Trismegistus' astrological teachings are based on the law that everything comes from the One, so everything is connected. "So seeing the cycles of the heavens, you can see the underlying cycles on earth because they're all following the same underlying spiritual cycle," Warnock explains. This belief refers to the Hermetic principle of correspondence: "As above, so below."

Some astrological generalities from *The Centiloquium of Hermes Trismegistus*: "The Sun and Moon next unto God, are the life of all things living."[107] In other words, the positions of the sun and moon in the sky at a person's time of birth can affect outcomes. This refers back to the Hermetic principle of gender in which the sun is the male gender and the moon female. Both are required to create all living things. *The Centiloquium of Hermes Trismegistus* also mentions retrograde planets and confirms the existence of twelve signs, "one of which is constantly ascending: the ascendant signifies the body, and the lord thereof the mind."[108]

The Centiloquium of Hermes Trismegistus states, "The judgments of astrologers are not many times true, by reason of the error of their instruments, or querents' ignorance" and warns practicing astrologers, "Be wary and circumspect in your judgment, when a fortune is with a malevolent; nor be you overconfident that the malice of the infortune shall

107. "The Classical Astrologer," *Classical Astrologer,* accessed July 26, 2021, https://classicalastrologer.me/hermes-trismegistus.
108. "The Classical Astrologer," https://classicalastrologer.me /hermes-trismegistus.

be averted."[109] Traditional astrological charts are extremely complex. "What you're doing is modeling reality. You're trying to have an accurate model of reality. And given the complexity of reality, the model has to be very complex too," Warnock declares.

Many people, especially in the West, where the attitude about astrology is that it is unscientific or false, often try to find problems to invalidate astrology. Warnock likens this viewpoint to one in which a doctor diagnoses a patient incorrectly or does not prescribe the right medication, so the doctor must be a fraud. "You would consider that to be a little irrational," he says. Economists use facts and figures to predict the future of the financial world, and their predictions do not always materialize. "But it comes from an accepted methodology. It's atheistic, materialistic. It's sort of scientific, so we accept it."

Astrology is based in mathematics and science, and during the Middle Ages and the Renaissance, many physicians studied astrology to help with medical diagnoses and treatment. Even today, astrologists are asked questions pertaining to health. "I'm not a doctor. It doesn't substitute for medical

109. "The Classical Astrologer," https://classicalastrologer.me /hermes-trismegistus.

advice. But I do medical order requests," Warnock states. "[I] can look at someone's natal chart and say what type of illnesses, how strong they are, how they're fatigued easily, what kind of typical illnesses they have over the course of their lifetime." Warnock says astrology is about technique. "But there's nevertheless a lot of judgment, intuition, and experience that's brought to bear as well."

Warnock has completed thousands of horary, or hourly, astrological charts, which are more traditional and focus on the celestial alignment at the time of a specific question. Although horary charts are not correct 100 percent of the time, they are generally accurate. "If that's true, then that means that the universe is not random," Warnock points out. "There is a spiritual connection of all things.…[T]he Hermetic model is correct or is at least a correct modeling. It's not to say that it's the only possible modeling, but it's not correct to say that everything is random and meaningless and pointless, and there is no pattern to things."

Translations of ancient astrological texts, as well as alchemy and magic texts, began popping up from 800 CE to 900 CE and then again from around 1200 CE to 1300 CE as Europe began to progress and become more sophisticated. Astrology became more simplified with each translation, but it has essentially kept its meaning. "Then with [the] Enlightenment," Warnock says, "basically people said astrology doesn't work, and so it was lost, so to speak. No one really practiced it. A few people did, and then probably around 1850 or so, it got revived and mostly as a natal." This natal astrology, based on a birth chart, is the most common version of today's modern astrology.

MODERN ASTROLOGY

Modern astrology includes twelve astrological signs, or sun signs, which describe the possible attributes and characteristics of the people born under these constellations in the zodiac. A person's astrological sign is based on the position of the sun in the zodiac on the person's date of birth. For example, if born in early September, the person's sign is Virgo because, based on the position of the earth, the sun was in the Virgo constellation on the date of birth. People born in late March have Aries as their sun sign. These twelve sun signs are the focus of modern astrology. These constellations of the zodiac were referred to in traditional astrology as well, in a more complex way.

Daily horoscopes can be found in newspapers, in magazines, and on the internet. These horoscopes generally describe the type of day one can expect, how one might feel that day, certain events that could happen, and so on.

Other factors that come into play with astrology are day and night charts, which are determined based on a person's birth time, date, and location, as well as ascendant signs, moon signs, and so on. These other factors are determined based on planetary, sun, moon, and star alignment. "A chart is a two-dimensional representation of a 3D reality for a specific time, date, and place," Warnock states. Warnock says astrology is a lot like gardening. For example, a gardener would not plant tomatoes in the winter but would plant based on the seasonal cycles. "If you understand the natural cycles and adapt yourself with them, and then take action, then you can have these miraculous results." A prediction based on astrology could guide a person to take action and make conscious decisions that could change the future.

"The reason sun signs are so popular is because it's extremely easy to figure them out. You only need to know the day [and] the month." The sun sign could be considered more important than the moon sign, but they work together to create significant insights into a person's life and experiences as a whole. There are twelve sun signs, but when the moon sign is added, the reading becomes more specific. "For example, the sun would be your basic personality. The moon would be your emotions," Warnock explains. Depending on where planets are located at a person's birth time, date, and location, they can affect certain attributes of the person's character. For example, the planet Mercury refers to thought, while Venus refers to relationships and creativity, and Mars drives anger. Jupiter relates to social relations, and Saturn refers to wisdom and judgment.

Depending on someone's date of birth, the person could also be born on the cusp, or a period of several days when the sun moves through two adjacent signs. This could mean the person has characteristics of both signs. "The thing about astrology, too, is that it has a great deal of judgment involved in it," Warnock declares. Interpretation depends on the experience and skill of the astrologist. Astrology also includes the human aspect, so if someone knows something is predicted to happen, that person can take steps to either avoid or create the incident.

"What's interesting to do is look at the natal charts, and you can see how the people sort of psychologically relate to each other," Warnock explains. Many people check astrological signs for compatibility within relationships, whether personal or professional. Based on thousands of years of research, many times these descriptions appear to be true.

TRADITIONAL ASTROLOGICAL SIGNS (SUN SIGNS)

Aries
March 21–April 19

Libra
September 23–October 22

Taurus
April 20–May 20

Scorpio
October 23–November 21

Gemini
May 21–June 20

Sagittarius
November 22–December 21

Cancer
June 21–July 22

Capricorn
December 22–January 19

Leo
July 23–August 22

Aquarius
January 20–February 18

Virgo
August 23–September 22

Pisces
February 19–March 20

Modern astrology is based on psychology, and sun sign horoscopes are mostly optimistic. Your daily horoscope might say to plan time to relax, offer a simple reminder to eat healthy and exercise, or suggest that if you stay on task, you will meet with great success. But with the traditional horary astrology that Warnock practices, the results are not always upbeat. "You really want to give an accurate answer," Warnock says, referring to what a chart might reveal regarding whether a person should marry or go into business with a specific person. Traditional astrology relies on traditional philosophy. "That was something that was important to me: to have a philosophical basis for [my practice]."

THE REEMERGENCE OF ASTROLOGY

There is more to astrology than what many might know about sun signs and modern horoscopes. Astrology has a long history, and in its complexity comprises various types found across the globe for the past several millennia. Even after researching and studying astrology for more than two decades, astrologist Christopher Warnock continues to educate himself about the practice. "I still think there's a lot of great, tremendous value in all the different types of astrology and very useful things that can be learned about it." Education about astrology—and in-depth education about any subject—is an endless journey. "What I would say about it is just to be open." A tremendous amount of information is available through literature, the internet, television, and so on. "It's a really wonderful time to be interested in astrology,"

Warnock says, "and all three Hermetic arts: astrology, alchemy, and magic."

Hermetic philosophies have influenced culture for several thousand years, and as Hermes Trismegistus' teachings come into prominence again in present time, a renaissance of culture could be on the horizon, leading to cultural developments. "We're going through some tough times now," Warnock states. "I think as a result of that, people are turning toward the necessity of having to become more spiritual."

Although bad things are bound to happen, these events could lead to blessings and open the door to better experiences. According to Hermetic teachings and the principle of rhythm, the pendulum will again swing toward the positive pole. Astrology is more or less focused on the fated aspect of life. "People hate fate. They want to have free will," Warnock declares. "Fate and free will [are] interesting because astrology would say that both are operating at the same time. That the underlying reality, the One, somehow transcends and incorporates both fate and free will, which is very odd. But it's neither one nor the other. It's both."

Chapter 15
ALCHEMY

Turning lead into gold. Achieving immortality. These notions might seem to exist only in fantasy, but they were at the center of the study of ancient alchemy. Many alchemists of old desired to turn metals into gold and discover everlasting life, but the main quest of these alchemists was to understand the natural world. Their experiments were based on scientific discovery, religion, and philosophy. Hermes Trismegistus is often called the father of alchemy, and his credited work *The Emerald Tablet of Hermes* is said to be one of the blueprints of early alchemists.

Although many believe alchemists simply held the implausible belief that they could discover a way to eternal life, much of the work of early alchemists laid the groundwork for modern-day science. They studied metals, minerals, and the human body to determine the inner workings of matter. Alchemists developed many techniques, methods, and tools, such as funnels and flasks, that are used in science labs today.

Alchemists used symbols to hide elemental meanings from those not privy to the information. These symbols often represent celestial bodies of astrology. In alchemy, the symbol for gold also represents the sun, and the symbol for silver also represents the moon. The secrets of alchemy in ancient times were known only to scholars of the subject. However, the practices and discoveries of alchemy led to modern-day chemistry, which is the study of matter.

ANCIENT ALCHEMY

Hermes Trismegistus is often called the founder or father of alchemy and astrology, and teacher of things mystical and magical. In ancient times, alchemy was thought to be magical by those who did not understand the study. "Anything that is considered high technology is always considered to be magical," comments Ja'Quintin Means, The Wondering Alchemist and author. Many believed ancient alchemists were working magic, but to the alchemists, they were simply trying to understand the natural world. Those who studied alchemy in ancient times theorized that it is possible to turn metal into gold or create eternal life. These theories failed but alchemists did discover how to transmute, or change, matter into things that would have beneficial physical, mental, and spiritual impacts.

"In the ancient world, there was no separation between magic, science, and religion. They were all the same. And today, we have a separation between the three," Means explains. "The reason that these old alchemists were able to make these scientific advances was because they were trying to find the secrets of nature, and they were trying to find the secrets of God and divinity and understand the universal laws and the laws of nature." Early alchemists were devout people, with a deep belief in the power of God. "They didn't want to be considered blasphemous by God. They wanted to make sure that everything they did was in accordance with the will of God."

There were two different approaches to alchemy in ancient times, inner and outer. The original form of alchemy is believed to have come from Egypt. "The name *alchemy* actually comes from the ancient word for Egypt, which is Kemet," Means explains. Kemet means "earth," or "black dirt," referring to the soil near the Nile. Adding *el* (*al*), which correlates with God, to the root word Kemet means one binds oneself to God. "The Egyptian people binding their physical vessels to God, or to the Divine," Means explains, "that's the inner view." Alchemists turning lead into gold was considered more of the outer world's view of alchemy.

Some alchemists were said to be con artists, promising tinctures to heal all wounds or offering to produce gold. For most alchemists, however, the real goal of alchemy was to perfect the soul. Means explains, "Getting one's soul so pure, through trials and tribulations, through the workings of just everyday life and the way that we treat each other, understanding certain spiritual aspects of life, not separating spirituality from any aspect of life: through that process of refinement, becoming gold ourselves because then you become one with the will of God or the will of the Divine."

Alchemists created charts so other alchemists could understand the meaning of each symbol. Using symbols to hide alchemical secrets not only protected the science and spirituality of the study from those who did not understand it, but also hid the meanings from the church. Most ancient alchemists believed you can become closer to God by refining your own soul. "They were basically saying you can become one with God without a pastor or a priest," Means explains.

Some examples of alchemy were creating tinctures to cure specific ailments or distilling liquids and materials into alcohol. Means, a professional brewer, considers himself a modern-day alchemist, as brewing is based on an ancient form of alchemy believed to have originated in Egypt thousands of years ago. Early alchemists are also associated with trying to discover or create the philosopher's stone, an unknown substance that can transmute metal into gold, heal wounds, or provide eternal life. Another belief of early alchemists is that a person who is perfected can become the philosopher's stone, attaining eternal life by becoming closer to God.

The Emerald Tablet of Hermes, credited to Hermes Trismegistus, is believed to be a blueprint for alchemists in their pursuit of a deeper understanding of everything and everyone. "I personally believe that it was people's desire to understand the world more," Means expresses, "that led to alchemy." Although some advances in science were made by early alchemists, many of the questions pondered by alchemists thousands of years ago are still being asked today. "We still question why are we here," Means says. "We still have these profound questions."

ALCHEMY CONSIDERED PRECURSOR TO CHEMISTRY

Alchemy was a precursor to modern chemistry, which is the study of matter and its properties. Alchemy was based on the traditional understanding that earth, water, air, and fire make up all matter. The knowledge and study of atoms, which constitute all matter, came much later. Eric Brentz has been teaching science for the past sixteen years, educating youth about the inner workings of matter. Atoms can be broken down into three subatomic particles: protons, electrons, and neutrons. "Those are tiny pieces that when they're separate, don't mean much. It's just a positive part, a negative part, and a neutral part," Brentz explains. "When you put them together in certain configurations, that's what makes up either elements, or when those elements combine with other elements, make up compounds that make up matter."

An atom is created when protons and neutrons coalesce and are forced together to form a nucleus, and then the electrons are attracted to the nucleus and begin bouncing around it. "We do understand why certain atoms will join together with other atoms, and that's based on their electron structure," Brentz points out. "Once a stable element is made, really the only part that can do anything, unless you force it through nuclear experiments, is the electrons." Above the single atom level, it is the electrons that pull other things to them to create matter. "That's how everything else in the world occurs....[H]ow we get everything that's made up of elements is the electrons joining together or sharing electrons."

The periodic table is an amazing advancement in the study of chemistry. Based on elemental studies, scientists realized all atoms are trying to accumulate a full shell of electrons in order to create. "Once you are above the single atom level, the electrons are the moneymaker. Those are the things that connect everything together," Brentz says. "If they interact with things that can help them do that, then that's how they form new compounds." For example, sodium and chlorine come together because they each want one thing the other can either give or take. They are separate elements, but when they are forced together, they create a new compound, salt.

Technology has improved, and within the past one hundred years, science has discovered even tinier particles, known as quarks, which make up protons, electrons, and neutrons. Science is ever evolving. Particle accelerators and controlled nuclear reactions have been used to split atoms. And although it is believed that all natural elements have been discovered, every so often new elements are discovered during these experiments and are added to the periodic table. These new elements, however, are unstable. "They're elements that only show up when we do these experiments, these extreme lab situations. Who knows where in the universe these elements show up naturally—if they even do?" Brentz questions.

Alchemists believed they could turn metals, such as lead, into gold. They used heat, chemicals, and basic lab processes of the time in an attempt to transmute metal into gold. They never succeeded. Modern scientists, however, have achieved this feat. Nuclear scientists, using particle accelerators, have been able to transmute metal into a small amount of gold. This proves the theory of early alchemists, but the modern-day experiments are not cost effective. The exorbitant amounts of money spent on these experiments could never be reimbursed through the creation of such a small amount of gold.

You do not need to be an alchemist or a chemist to experiment and see a difference in matter. "Probably the best chemical to use is water," Brentz explains. Water (H_2O) is formed when two hydrogen atoms and one oxygen atom combine to create a molecular compound. If you drop a dusty rock into a cup of water, a mixture of dirt and water may be created, but this is not a chemical reaction. But if you drop tablets of antacid into a glass of water, a chemical reaction will occur. "They fizz because the electrons in the calcium that is in the antacid reacts with the water, and atoms get traded between those two things, and it forms bubbles," Brentz explains. "That's how you can tell that's a chemical reaction happening—because the bubbles weren't there before." It creates a new compound. But if you mix soap and water together, resulting in bubbles, that is not a chemical reaction. The bubbles are a property of the soap, so it is not a new compound or matter; it is simply a mixture of soap and water. A chemical reaction can also be observed when charcoal is lit on fire. Charcoal is basically condensed carbon, and once heat is added, it turns gray and releases smoke. These are signs of chemical changes.

"Our entire existence is based on chemistry because of all our digestive processes and cellular processes that actually take chemical reactions to keep going," Brentz says. Science, even if incorrect or incomplete at times, can lead to future developments. For example, at one point, scientists could not prove the existence of atoms. Brentz points out, "It's important to realize how wrong we may have been but what was right or what could be useful in those earlier theories."

Although some of what early alchemists believed is disproven by modern science, alchemy should be recognized as an important study. The evolution of science continues in present time. When it comes to science, people want clear-cut answers, but these are not always possible. The recommendations of today may not be conclusive tomorrow, as information and implementation change. "It's okay for science to be wrong, especially when we are going off limited data," Brentz says. "Science is always evolving, and a lot of it is ambiguous. And that's hard for us because science is so important to our lives. We would like it to be more cut-and-dry. Certainly, there are some rules and some laws about science that are fairly cut-and-dry, but it is, as a process, constantly evolving."

THE "MAGIC" OF ALCHEMY

Much of science might appear to be magical or mystical. It is difficult to understand the true inner workings of how chemistry, physics, biology, and so on, actually operate. For example, the process of turning waves into videos and sounds on a television is a mystery to most, but for the discoverers and developers of this process, it is comprehensible.

Most people are unable to see what is happening in the universe at the atomic level, so it appears magical.

Scientists of ancient times pursued the study and practice of alchemy, as scientists do in their chosen fields today, in hopes of learning more about how matter and energy work. The efforts of these early scientists benefited society and led to a deeper understanding of the universe and all things in it.

Chapter 16

MAGIC

What comes to mind when you ponder the idea of magic? You might revert back to the idea that magic is a practice of the occult, darkness, and demons. Or you might veer toward a more positive view of magic. Perhaps you think of the supernatural work of God and angels to produce true miracles. Some may think magic is using natural ingredients to create medicinal teas or casting simple spells to bring peace to those in mourning. Others may say magic is using crystal balls or summoning spirits for knowledge of the future. Still others might think of magicians on a Vegas stage practicing tricks of illusion. According to *Encyclopaedia Britannica*, magic includes an array of practices ranging from divination and incantations to astrology, alchemy, sorcery, and slight-of-hand tricks.[110]

---

110. Robert Andrew Gilbert, "Magic," *Encyclopaedia Britannica*, accessed July 20, 2021, https://www.britannica.com/topic/magic-supernatural-phenomenon.

"The purpose of magic is to acquire knowledge, power, love, or wealth; to heal or ward off illness or danger; to guarantee productivity or success in an endeavour; to cause harm to an enemy; to reveal information; to induce spiritual transformation; to trick; or to entertain."[111] With such a variety of magical purposes, you may get confused about the true meaning of magic.

So what is magic? According to a definition in *Merriam-Webster*, magic is "an extraordinary power or influence seemingly from a supernatural source."[112] The belief in magic and the supernatural has been around for thousands of years, and if you look for magical blessings, then you will find them in ordinary experiences.

MAGIC OF ANCIENT TIMES

In the ancient times of Hermes Trismegistus, magic was a part of life, just as was science, religion, and philosophy.

---

111. Robert Andrew Gilbert, "History of Magic in Western Worldviews," *Encyclopaedia Britannica*, accessed July 30, 2021, https://www.britannica.com/topic/magic-supernatural-phenomenon/History-of-magic-in-Western-worldviews.
112. "Magic," *Merriam-Webster*, accessed July 30, 2021, https://www.merriam-webster.com/dictionary/magic.

Throughout Trismegistus' writings, many of his statements appear to be magical or supernatural in nature. If something is not fully understood, some may label it magical. Even with an understanding of how something works, such as the human body, some may believe it to be truly magical in nature. Belief is about both knowledge and perception.

Much magic went hand in hand with the scientific method of ancient times. Alchemists experimented to prove hypotheses at different times of the day, possibly at midnight or during a full moon, in hopes of discovering different outcomes. They combined different ingredients to create tinctures, which some call potions.

Tess Muin-Bruneau, interfaith minister, tarot reader, and the witch behind Witch's Chamber, an online business specializing in handcrafted jewelry and decorative accessories, says that in ancient times, magic was more acceptable and was practiced in everyday life. Practitioners of ancient times were more respected and valued. "There were those that knew the magic of the elements and shared to protect their circles, [from] using a plant to cure an ailment to tapping into the energy of the earth to shield your village from bad weather," Muin-Bruneau states. As Christianity spread, the practice of magic became less acceptable.

The Salem witch trials took place in the late 1600s. Beginning prior to these trials and concurrent with them, a witch hunt spread across Europe. In Salem, Massachusetts, about two hundred people, mostly women, were accused of witchcraft and conspiring with the devil. Nearly two dozen people died during the Salem witch trials, either by hanging or while awaiting trial in jail. One man died as a result of heavy rocks being placed on his body. The courts later realized their error and cleared the accused and the convicted of the supernatural charges against them.

The concept of magic has shifted over time. What is magic? This question can generate different responses from different people based on their knowledge, beliefs, and perception. "I think just as magic can show up in so many different ways to different people, that is exactly how many different views exist on magic," Muin-Bruneau says.

MAGIC TODAY

A negative view of magic in modern times could stem from religious beliefs or Hollywood's depiction of evil witches and warlocks and of vengeful gods and spirits. But tales of witchcraft and wizardry, narratives of heroes with supernatural gifts, and stories of people communing with spirits to bring relief to grieving loved ones fill books and screens in today's world. Despite the fact that most of the magic people read about or watch is fiction, true magic is considered by some to be at work in everyone and everything.

"Magic is alive. It lives and breathes all around us, all the time," shares Muin-Bruneau. "It is a vibration, at times a current, you can feel running through you, a connection to all that was, is, and will be." The notion of energy connecting everyone and everything refers back to the Hermetic principle of vibration. Muin-Bruneau believes magic is this energy that connects all of life. Your vibration can affect how you connect with others, how you think, and how you feel. Muin-Bruneau points out, "Depending on how your own personal vibration, [or] magic, connects to the universal can and will change your life. It is a sacred agreement with the universe to respect and work with its laws of energy."

Magic is the energy of manifestation. Do you want to see more magic in your life? Start simple. "Learn to work with your own rhythms. Spend time in nature, try walking barefoot in the soil, let yourself feel the connection and grounding," Muin-Bruneau suggests. Experiencing magic is different for everyone. "Understand that everything and everyone you meet has their own magic, so be aware of the energy you send out, as magic is energy and energy returns," Muin-Bruneau states. "Hold on, breathe, and believe in your own magic. There is nothing stronger than that."

SEE THE MAGIC IN EVERYTHING

Perception and belief play important roles in finding magic in everyday life. You could simply sit and experience the magic of nature outdoors as the cool breeze blows, the birds chirp, and the sun warms your body. You could see magic in the smile of a child, the love between a couple celebrating fifty years together, or the first steps of a person learning to walk again after a tragedy. Magic could be experienced in the answer to a prayer, a kind word from a stranger, or the fragrance of a flower. Magic is everywhere if you just take the time to embrace it. "It is being at the right place at the right time, finding the perfect whatever-it-is-you-are-looking-for just when you need it," says Muin-Bruneau. "Even waking up daily is magic."

Magic can be found in the simplest or most complex situations. "You just need to be willing to see it, and it will manifest for you," Muin-Bruneau explains. If you choose to become more aware and conscious of what is actually happening around you, magic is easy to see. These magical energies can help connect you to others and allow you to experience the blessings of everyday life.

Chapter 17

WE ARE ALL IN THIS TOGETHER

Most—perhaps all—religions and belief systems across the globe have a verse, or Golden Rule, that says to treat others how you wish to be treated.

GOLDEN RULES OF RELIGIONS[113]

Buddhism: Treat not others in ways that you yourself would find hurtful.

Christianity: Do unto others as you would have them do unto you.

---

113. Paul McKenna, "The Golden Rule Across the World's Religions: Thirteen Sacred Texts," Scarboro Missions, 2000, https://static1.squarespace.com/static/5852af6a579fb39b66b 50478/t/5caf993c652dea8557e6a38a/1555011900715/The+ Golden+Rule+Across+the+World.pdf.

Hinduism: This is the sum of duty: do not do to others what would cause pain if done to you.

Islam: Not one of you truly believes until you wish for others what you wish for yourself.

Judaism: What is hateful to you, do not do to your neighbour. This is the whole Torah; all the rest is commentary. Go and learn it.

Sikhism: I am a stranger to no one; and no one is a stranger to me. Indeed, I am a friend to all.

Taoism: Regard your neighbor's gain as your own gain and your neighbor's loss as your own loss.

The list continues. If this is the rule or principle of theologies and beliefs among cultures across the globe, how can humanity learn to come together with the understanding that each individual is part of the collective whole, that we are all connected to one another? If you believe in a higher power, God, the Source, THE ALL, or even the higher consciousness of your own mind, you should find that the answer is what has been said throughout millennia. This may not always be easy, but if you are self-aware and realize that other people are dealing with their own emotions and working to overcome trauma, heartache, anxiety, impatience, and so on, then it may be easier to accept a situation as it actually is instead of how you might otherwise perceive it. Keep safety in mind when you are involved in a divisive situation. The best thing to do might be to remove yourself from such a situation. But discussion could resume at a later time, when all parties are calmer.

We are all in this life together. Everything and everyone on this planet, according to Hermeticism and theologies and beliefs passed down for generations, came from THE ALL, the One, God, the Source, the Creator, and so on. Everyone is part of the energy and the collective mind of the universe. If you understand this and become more conscious and self-aware, then it may be easier to see others as they are in this time and space.

For many, a shift of knowledge is on the horizon. Many yearn for a true connection to those around them, to nature, and to a higher power. Many have questions about their existence in this realm. Many are awakening to the awe of amazing events experienced on this earth—perhaps the beauty of the morning sunrise over a dew-covered field, the perfection of a colorful rainbow after the storm, or the carefree laughter of a child. Many believe that energy is within all things, and spirituality can bring them closer to enlightenment. With this shift in consciousness, many are searching for a deeper understanding of their place in this expansive existence and for answers to where and why they belong in this time and space.

With the information shared in this book regarding the Hermetic principles at work in everyday life, you will find guidance and information on how to develop a deeper understanding of the mind, body, and spirit. Many are on a personal journey of self-discovery to find true purpose. By becoming a lifelong learner, you can continuously improve your knowledge about spirituality, energy, and the interconnectedness of everyone and everything. This book has been written at this moment in time to share the knowledge of Hermes Trismegistus and to help those who hear this message learn to live life to the fullest.

BIBLIOGRAPHY

Brentz, Eric (Texas public school educator), in discussion with the author, July 2021.

Brown, Brené. *Daring Greatly: How the Courage to Be Vulnerable Transforms the Way We Live, Love, Parent, and Lead.* New York: Gotham Books, 2012.

Brown, Les. *Success.* "The Story You Believe about Yourself Determines Your Success." YouTube video. October 8, 2017. https://www.youtube.com/watch?v=68Wz25NMX2k.

Brown, Kirk, and Richard Ryan. "The Benefits of Being Present: Mindfulness and Its Role in Psychological Well-Being." *Journal of Personality and Social Psychology* 84, no. 4 (2003): 822–48. https://doi.org/10.1037/0022-3514.84.4.822.

"The Classical Astrologer." *Classical Astrologer.* Accessed July 26, 2021. https://classicalastrologer.me/hermes-trismegistus.

Corbett, Tom, and Lady Stearn Robinson. *The Dreamer's Dictionary: From A to Z...3,000 Magical Mirrors to Reveal the Meaning of Your Dreams.* New York: Warner Books, 1994.

Darvischi, Summer (owner of Open Hearts Yoga Sanctuary and Open Hearts Crystal Blessings), in discussion with the author, June 2021.

Dweck, Carol S. *Mindset: The New Psychology of Success.* New York: Ballantine Books, 2008.

Emmons, Robert A., and Michael E. McCullough. "Counting Blessings Versus Burdens: An Experimental Investigation of Gratitude and Subjective Well-Being in Daily Life." *Journal of Personality and Social Psychology* 84, no. 2 (2003): 377–89. https://doi.org/10.1037/0022-3514.84.2.377.

Francis, Charles (director of the Mindfulness Meditation Institute and author of *Mindfulness Meditation Made Simple*), in discussion with the author, June 2021.

Freud, Sigmund. *The Interpretations of Dreams.* New York: The Macmillan Company, 1913.

Gilbert, Robert Andrew. "History of Magic in Western Worldviews." *Encyclopaedia Britannica.* Accessed July 30, 2021. https://www.britannica.com/topic/magic-supernatural -phenomenon/History-of-magic-in-Western-worldviews.

Gilbert, Robert Andrew. "Magic." *Encyclopaedia Britannica.* Accessed July 20, 2021. https://www.britannica.com/topic /magic-supernatural-phenomenon.

Hall, Charlie, PhD (professor in the Department of Horticultural Sciences at Texas A&M University and holder of the Ellison Chair in International Floriculture), in discussion with the author, June 2021.

Hall, Manly P., 33rd degree Freemason, "The Hermetic Philosophy" (full lecture/clean audio). YouTube video. July 4, 2019. MindPodNetwork, https://www.youtube.com /watch?v=P0LMh2bHNz0.

Harvey, Steve. *The Official Steve Harvey.* "Imagination Is Every-thing" (Motivated + Steve Harvey). YouTube video. June 10,

2019. https://www.youtube.com/watch?v=TbEMIw3ec
GI&list=PLh9wooqH0eenSRQmZLz8dwhzVqTUtqvCL.

The Holy Bible, King James Version. Nashville: Tennessee: Thomas
Nelson Publishers, 1989.

Krznaric, Roman. "Six Habits of Highly Empathetic
People." *Greater Good Magazine*. November 27, 2012.
https://greatergood.berkeley.edu/article/item/six_habits
_of_highly_empathic_people1.

Layden, Lisa (thought leader), in discussion with the author, June
2021.

McCraty, Rollin, PhD (director of research at HeartMath®, Inc.),
in discussion with the author, June 2021.

McKenna, Paul. "The Golden Rule Across the World's Religions:
Thirteen Sacred Texts." Scarboro Missions. 2000. https://
static1.squarespace.com/static/5852af6a579fb39b66b50478
/t/5caf993c652dea8557e6a38a/1555011900715
/The+Golden+Rule+Across+the+World.pdf.

Means, Ja'Quintin (The Wondering Alchemist and author of
Thoughts of a Prince), in discussion with the author, July 2021.

Merriam-Webster. "Magic." Accessed July 30, 2021.
https://www.merriam-webster.com/dictionary/magic.

Muin-Bruneau, Tess (interfaith minister, tarot reader, and the
witch behind Witch's Chamber), in an email interview with the
author, July 2021.

Parten, Jenny (Reiki master and medicine woman), in discussion
with the author, June 2021.

Penberthy, Jennifer Kim, PhD, ABPP (board certified licensed
clinical psychologist, Chester F. Carlson Professor of Psychiatry

and Neurobehavioral Sciences at the University of Virginia School of Medicine), in discussion with the author, July 2021.

Register, Dena, PhD, MT-BC (regulatory affairs advisor for the Certification Board for Music Therapists), in discussion with the author, July 2021.

Robbins, Tony. "Where Focus Goes, Energy Flows." YouTube video. January 17, 2017. https://www.youtube.com /watch?v=Z6nv26BTzKA.

Rose, Joree, MA, LMFT (owner of the Mindfulness and Therapy Center and author of *A Year of Gratitude*), in discussion with the author, July 2021.

Samman, Mendy (master black belt in American karate and master personal trainer), in discussion with the author, June 2021.

Shearer, Ryan (believer of Jesus the Messiah), in discussion with the author, July 2021.

The Three Initiates. *The Kybalion: A Study of the Hermetic Philosophy of Ancient Egypt and Greece*. Chicago: The Yogi Publication Society, 1908.

Trismegistus, Hermes. *The Corpus Hermeticum: Initiation Into Hermetics, The Hermetica of Hermes Trismegistus*. Translated by G. R. S. Mead. Pantianos Classics, 1906.

Trismegistus, Hermes. *The Divine Pymander and Other Writings of Hermes Trismegistus*. Translated by John D. Chambers. Eastford, Connecticut: Martino Fine Books, 2018.

Trismegistus, Hermes. *The Emerald Tablet of Hermes*. Translated by multiple translators. Los Angeles: Merchant Books, 2013.

Trismegistus, Hermes. *Thrice-Greatest Hermes: Studies in Hellenistic Theosophy and Gnosis (three volumes in one)*. Translated by G. R. S. Mead. Mansfield Centre, Connecticut: Martino Publishing, 2013.

Ulrich, Roger S. "View from a Window May Influence Recovery from Surgery." *Science* 224, no. 4647 (1984): 420–21. https://www.jstor.org/stable/1692984.

US Energy Information Administration. "What Is Energy? Laws of Energy." Accessed June 29, 2021. https://www.eia.gov/energyexplained/what-is-energy/laws-of-energy.php.

Warnock, Christopher (traditional astrologer and author of *Secrets of Planetary Magic*), in discussion with the author, June 2021.

ACKNOWLEDGMENTS

They say it takes a village to raise a child. I say, it takes a village to write a book! Without the insight of those who shared their ideas and expertise, *The Little Book of Hermetic Principles* would never have materialized. I owe each of these experts a debt of gratitude and appreciation for aiding me throughout my journey to share the ancient knowledge of Hermes Trismegistus and how you can take steps to benefit from these principles, ultimately experiencing personal growth and self-awareness to deepen your understanding of mind, body, and spirit.

As the author of *The Little Book of Hermetic Principles*, I would like to express my gratitude to the following people for allowing me to share their knowledge with readers. I appreciate you!

To Eric Brentz, I appreciate the analysis of chemistry and our time spent together teaching young minds.

To Summer Darvischi, thanks for sharing your expertise in the healing powers of crystals.

To Charles Francis, thank you for sharing your knowledge and tips on how readers can incorporate mindfulness meditation into daily life.

To Charlie Hall, PhD, I appreciate you sharing your expertise with and insight into the natural world and how we can benefit from our own experiences with Mother Nature.

To Lisa Layden, I thank you for your insight into the importance of finding true purpose in this life and understanding that we are all part of a collective whole.

To Rollin McCraty, PhD, I appreciate you taking time to share the eye-opening benefits of HeartMath®.

To Ja'Quintin Means, thank you for sharing your knowledge about the world of ancient alchemy and those who practiced it.

To Tess Muin-Bruneau, I thank you for your insight into how we can see the magic in all things.

To Jenny Parten, thank you for sharing your insight into the power of raising energetic frequencies and for helping guide me on my journey of self-discovery.

To Jennifer Kim Penberthy, PhD, ABPP, thank you for sharing the importance of mental health and tips on how to learn to thrive.

To Dena Register, PhD, MT-BC, your insight into the benefits of music is inspiring and appreciated.

To Joree Rose, MA, LMFT, thank you for sharing your tips on how to become more assertive and for sharing your journey.

To Mendy Samman, thank you for sharing your expertise in the mental and physical benefits of exercise, as well as helping me during my fitness journey.

To Ryan Shearer, I appreciate you sharing your firsthand experience of witnessing God's work and the benefits of prayer. I am grateful for your friendship.

To Christopher Warnock, your knowledge of all things astrology is appreciated, and I thank you.

I would also like to share my appreciation of the following people.

To my acquisitions editor, Claire Sielaff, and my publisher, Ulysses Press, thank you for taking a chance on me. To Renee Rutledge, my editor, thank you for your support and guid-

ance throughout the editing process. To Kathy Kaiser, my copyeditor, I owe a debt of gratitude for your thoroughness in fine-tuning my words. And to everyone on the production team, thank you for your diligent work on this book.

To the reader, thank you for spending your valuable time absorbing this information. I truly hope you have found some beneficial knowledge within the pages of this book. I wish you well.

To my parents, Gary and Beverly Morris, thank you for your continuous support.

To my husband, Tristan Browne, and my children, Mia and Dane, I love you and appreciate you for simply existing and interacting with me in my world.

I must also thank God for providing this book-writing opportunity to me. It is a lifelong dream come true.

I truly believe that through education and awareness, we can all learn from one another and grow as individuals, as well as a collective whole. Understanding the connectedness of everything and everyone around us can lead to a shift in society. I believe that with more self-awareness and conscious action, people can learn to increase their vibration, or energy, and live happier, more fulfilling lives.

ABOUT THE AUTHOR

Amber D. Browne is a lifelong writer and communicator. As a young teen, she discovered her passion for the written word and a purpose of sharing information. After acquiring a BA in mass communication from Southwest Texas State University, since renamed Texas State University, Amber spent much of her career researching and reporting Texas news for radio. She later branched out as a freelance writer and editor for local magazines, and her desire to share her journalism experience led to a seven-year stint in junior high education as an English language arts/reading and media teacher. Amber resides in the Dallas-Fort Worth metroplex with her husband and their two children. Find more of Amber's written work at www.amberdbrowne.com.